PASSWORD 1

THIRD EDITION

A READING AND VOCABULARY TEXT

Linda Butler

To Suzanne, with love

Password 1: A Reading and Vocabulary Text
Third Edition

Copyright © 2017 by Pearson Education, Inc. or its affiliates.

All rights reserved. Printed in the United States of America. This publication is protected
by copyright, and permission should be obtained from the publisher prior to any prohibited
reproduction, storage in a retrieval system, or transmission in any form or by any means,
electronic, mechanical, photocopying, recording, or otherwise. For information regarding
permissions, request forms and the appropriate contacts within the Pearson Education Global
Rights & Permissions department, please visit wwww.pearsoned.com/permissions.

Unless otherwise indicated herein, any third-party trademarks that may appear in this work
are the property of their respective owners and any references to third-party trademarks,
logos or other trade dress are for demonstrative or descriptive purposes only. Such references
are not intended to imply any sponsorship, endorsement, authorization, or promotion of
Pearson's products by the owners of such marks, or any relationship between the owner and
Pearson Education, Inc. or its affiliates, authors, licensees or distributors.

Pearson Education, 221 River Street, Hoboken, NJ 07030

Staff credits: The people who made up the *Password* team, representing editorial,
production, design, and manufacturing, are Pietro Alongi, Claire Bowers, Tracey Cataldo,
Mindy DePalma, Dave Dickey, Warren Fischbach, Pam Fishman, Niki Lee, Amy McCormick,
Robert Ruvo, Kristina Skof, and Joseph Vella.

Development Editor: Penny Laporte
Cover image: Pairat Pinijkul / Shutterstock
Text composition: ElectraGraphics, Inc.

Library of Congress Cataloging-in-Publication Data
A catalog record for the print edition is available from the Library of Congress.
ISBN-10: 0-13-439934-X   ISBN-13: 978-0-13-439934-8

Printed in the United States of America
ScoutAutomatedPrintCode

39 2025

CONTENTS

SCOPE AND SEQUENCE

Unit/Chapter	Developing Reading Skills	Learning Target Vocabulary	Using Critical Thinking	Practicing Writing
UNIT 1 LEARNING SOMETHING NEW				
Chapter 1: *Mayda Learns to Swim* page 2	• Identifying the topic of a reading • Recognizing the main idea • Remembering details • Completing a summary **Tips** • Reading a passage several times • Reading for main idea and details	*afraid, because, beginner, every, extra, feeling, practice, ready* **Tips** • Knowing alphabetical order	• **Identifying** reasons • **Making inferences** • **Citing evidence** from the text • **Supporting** your opinion **Tips** • Using critical thinking skills	• Using target vocabulary in sentences • Doing a dictation • Writing sentences about yourself **Tips** • Using *afraid* in sentences
Chapter 2: *Learning to Make Movies* page 9	• Identifying the topic of a reading • Recognizing the main idea • Remembering details • Completing a summary **Tips** • What a title can tell you	*busy, everything, favorite, just, more , other, too , use* **Tips** • Definition of *phrase*	• **Citing evidence** from the text • **Analyzing** a text • **Making inferences** • **Drawing parallels** **Tips** • Making guesses to infer meaning	• Using target vocabulary in sentences • Doing a dictation • Writing sentences about favorite people and things **Tips** • Reading aloud to check your writing
Chapter 3: *Finding Time for Everything* page 17	• Identifying the topic of a reading • Recognizing the main idea • Scanning • Building a summary **Tips** • Keeping your head still when you read	*a few, early, enough, for example, have to, spend, tired, well* **Tips** • Finding words in the dictionary • Using *spend*	• **Drawing examples** from the text • **Evaluating** the writer's opinion • Understanding **text features** • **Interpreting** words based on the context **Tips** • Reacting to the writer's opinion	• Using target vocabulary in sentences • Doing a dictation • Writing sentences about your weekends **Tips** • Writing extra sentences for practice
Unit 1 *Checkpoint* Page 24	• Look Back • Reviewing Vocabulary • Expanding Vocabulary: Words with *every-* • A Puzzle • Extra Reading: *Learning to Drive* Comprehension Check, Scanning, The Topic and the Main Idea, Critical Thinking			
UNIT 2 I'M HUNGRY! ARE YOU?				
Chapter 4: *The Job of a Food Critic* page 30	• Identifying the topic of a reading • Recognizing the main idea • Remembering details • Completing a summary **Tips** • Reading for the main idea and details	*also, detail, kind, maybe, most, smell, the same, would like* **Tips** • Using *would like*	• **Evaluating** information in a text • **Citing evidence** from a text • **Expanding on information** in a text • **Making inferences** **Tips** • Identifying the writer's reasons for an opinion	• Using target vocabulary in sentences • Doing a dictation • Writing sentences about a restaurant **Tips** • Using *also* and *too*
Chapter 5: *Who Likes Cereal?* page 37	• Identifying the topic of a reading • Recognizing the main idea • Remembering details • Building a summary	*bowl, box, breakfast, lunch, may, meal, quick, snack* **Tips** • The meaning of *definition* • The meaning of *may* and *might*	• **Applying information** from a text • **Interpreting a circle graph** • **Synthesizing** information from a text • **Making inferences** **Tips** • Answering questions by considering the options • The meaning of circle graphs (pie charts)	• Using target vocabulary in sentences • Doing a dictation • Writing sentences about your favorite meal **Tips** • Using *may* and *maybe*

Unit/Chapter	Developing Reading Skills	Learning Target Vocabulary	Using Critical Thinking	Practicing Writing
Chapter 6: *Healthy Eating* **page 44**	• Scanning • Understanding pronoun reference • Building a summary **Tips** • Avoiding vocalizing when you read	*different, group, grow, information, plan, really, show, size* **Tips** • Using *group*	• **Noticing** the language used in a text • **Categorizing information** from a text • **Applying information** from a text • **Analyzing** the text **Tips** • Supporting your opinion with reasons	• Using target vocabulary in sentences • Doing a dictation • Writing sentences about foods you do and don't like **Tips** • Using *or* and *and*
Unit 2 *Checkpoint* **page 52**	• Look Back • Reviewing Vocabulary • Expanding Vocabulary: The suffix *-er* • A Puzzle • Extra Reading: *Popcorn* Comprehension Check, Scanning, The Main Idea, Critical Thinking			

UNIT 3   HAVING FUN

Unit/Chapter	Developing Reading Skills	Learning Target Vocabulary	Using Critical Thinking	Practicing Writing
Chapter 7: *An Easy Game* **page 62**	• Identifying the topic of a reading • Recognizing the main idea • Scanning • Using a diagram **Tips** • Avoiding translating as you read	*around, beat, both, decide, each, hold, rule, stand, try, world* **Tips** • Meanings of *around* • *Both* and *all*	• **Making inferences** • **Synthesizing** information from a text • **Interpreting** a photo based on information in a text • Understanding a **writer's purpose** **Tips** • Diagramming information from a text	• Using target vocabulary in sentences • Doing a dictation • Writing sentences about games
Chapter 8: *A New and Different Sport* **page 69**	• Identifying the topic of a reading • Recognizing the main idea • Giving details • Completing a summary **Tips** • Seeing words in groups as you read	*agree, catch, continue, enjoy, field, happen, problem, seem, somewhere, team* **Tips** • Opposite meanings: *Agree* and *disagree* • The meaning of *somewhere*	• **Making comparisons** with a Venn diagram • **Applying a concept** from the text • **Supporting your opinion** • **Citing evidence** from the text **Tips** • Making comparisons with a Venn diagram	• Using target vocabulary in sentences • Doing a dictation • Writing sentences about sports
Chapter 9: *Collectors* **page 76**	• Identifying the topic of a reading • Recognizing the main idea • Citing examples • Giving details	*care, carry, collect, hope, laugh, only, pick up, remember, together, without* **Tips** • The meaning of *collector* and *collection* • Synonyms: *only* and *just* • The meaning of *carry*	• **Interpreting** language used in a text • **Citing reasons** • **Identifying** main ideas and supporting details • **Responding** to the writer's opinion **Tips** • Supporting your opinion with examples	• Using target vocabulary in sentences • Doing a dictation • Writing sentences about your own experiences **Tips** • Using *care about*
Unit 3 *Checkpoint* **page 84**	• Look Back • Reviewing Vocabulary • Expanding Vocabulary: Nouns • A Puzzle • Extra Reading: *Do You Like Puzzles?* Comprehension Check, Scanning, Topics of Paragraphs, The Main Idea, Critical Thinking			

UNIT 4   FRIENDS

Unit/Chapter	Developing Reading Skills	Learning Target Vocabulary	Using Critical Thinking	Practicing Writing
Chapter 10: *Good Friends and Good Health* **page 92**	• Identifying the topic of a reading • Recognizing the main idea • Identifying topics of paragraphs • Reading for details **Tips** • The purpose of a bulleted list	*get, health, heart, if, life, often, sad, strong, surprise, understand* **Tips** • Meaning of *get* + noun or adjective • *Life* and *lives*	• Understanding **comparisons** • **Citing examples** from the text • **Analyzing** the text • **Posing questions** on the topic **Tips** • Comparing two people or things	• Using target vocabulary in sentences • Writing a paragraph about time with your friends **Tips** • Giving opinions with *I (don't) think*

Unit/Chapter	Developing Reading Skills	Learning Target Vocabulary	Using Critical Thinking	Practicing Writing
Chapter 11: *Being Honest with Friends* page 100	• Identifying the topic of a reading • Recognizing the main idea • Understanding sentences with because • Reading for details **Tips** • Marking important information	*angry , better, careful, difficult, hurt , should , so, tell the truth, trust, worry* **Tips** • *Hurt* as a verb or adjective • Using *better*	• Determining **pronoun reference** • **Comparing** definitions • **Supporting your opinion** • **Making predictions** based on a text	• Using target vocabulary in sentences • Writing a paragraph about telling friends the truth **Tips** • Using *should (not)* to give an opinion
Chapter 12: *Are Online Friends Real Friends?* page 108	• Identifying the topic of a reading • Recognizing the main idea • Understanding pronoun reference • Understanding sentences with because **Tips** • Meanings of the pronoun *you*	*choose, close, each other , future, go on, interested in, mistake, safe, too, wrong* **Tips** • Meanings of *go on* • Meaning of *make a mistake*	• **Synthesizing** information from a text • **Making predictions** based on a text • **Organizing** information in a T-chart • **Supporting your opinion** **Tips** • Using a T-chart	• Using target vocabulary in sentences • Writing a paragraph about online friends **Tips** • Using *interested in* • Supporting the main idea of a paragraph
Unit 4 *Checkpoint* page 115	• Look Back • Reviewing Vocabulary • Expanding Vocabulary: Verbs • A Puzzle • Extra Reading: *Pets as Friends* Comprehension Check, Sentences with *Because*, The Topic and the Main Idea, Critical Thinking			

UNIT 5 ON THE JOB

Unit/Chapter	Developing Reading Skills	Learning Target Vocabulary	Using Critical Thinking	Practicing Writing
Chapter 13: *Working Teens* page 126	• Identifying the topic of a reading • Recognizing the main idea • Reading for details • Recognizing facts vs. opinions **Tips** • Using italics for emphasis	*between, during, expensive, fact, half, let's, make money, parent, relationship, save* **Tips** • Meaning of *parents* and *relatives*	• **Synthesizing** information from a text • **Organizing** information in a T-chart • **Making inferences** • **Supporting your opinion** **Tips** • Determining the writer's opinion	• Using target vocabulary in sentences • Writing a paragraph about high school students working **Tips** • Writing titles • Supporting your opinion with reasons
Chapter 14: *Night Work* page 134	• Identifying the topic of a reading • Recognizing the main idea • Reading for details • Recognizing facts vs. opinions **Tips** • Quotations in a text	*accident , body, company, forget, hard , leave, machine, mean, shift, stress* **Tips** • Meaning of *shift* • *Leave* with or without an object	• **Interpreting** language used in a text • **Prioritizing reasons** given in a text • **Applying** information from a text • **Supporting your opinion**	• Using target vocabulary in sentences • Writing a paragraph about yourself **Tips** • Using *leave for* + a destination
Chapter 15: *Working for Tips* page 142	• Identifying the topic of a reading • Recognizing the main idea • Reading for details • Completing a summary **Tips** • Noticing definitions in a text	*believe, bill, change, expect, fair, interesting, large, over, soon, sure* **Tips** • Using *interesting* and *interested in* • Meanings of *change*	• **Interpreting** language used in the text • **Citing evidence** from a text • **Recognizing** facts vs. opinions • **Making inferences**	• Using target vocabulary in sentences • Writing a paragraph about working for tips
Unit 5 *Checkpoint* page 149	• Look Back • Reviewing Vocabulary • Expanding Vocabulary: Adjectives • A Puzzle • Extra Reading: *Help for Working Parents* Comprehension Check, Reading for Details, Fact vs. Opinion, The Main Idea, Critical Thinking			

THE THIRD EDITION OF THE *PASSWORD* SERIES

Welcome to the third edition of *Password*, a series designed to help learners of English develop their English-language reading skills and expand their vocabularies. The series offers theme-based units which include:

- engaging nonfiction reading passages,
- a variety of activities to develop reading and critical thinking skills, and
- exercises to help students understand, remember, and use new words and phrases.

Each book in the *Password* series can be used independently of the others, but when used as a series, the books will help students reach the 2,000-word vocabulary level, at which point, research has shown, learners can begin to read unadapted texts.

The *Password* approach to reading skill development for English-language learners is based on the following ideas:

1. The best way for learners to develop their English reading skills is to read English-language materials at an appropriate level.

Attractive, high-interest materials will spark learners' motivation to read, but to sustain that motivation, "second language reading instruction must find ways to avoid continually frustrating the reader."[1] Learners of English need reading materials at an appropriate level of difficulty, materials that do not reduce them to struggling to decipher a puzzle. Materials at an inappropriate level will not allow learners to develop reading strategies but rather will discourage them from reading.

The level of difficulty of ELT materials is determined by many factors, such as the learner's familiarity with the topic, the learner's L1 reading skills, the length and structure of the words, sentences, and paragraphs, and the structure of the text as a whole. These are among the factors that influence the construction of all good ELT reading materials and the way they gradually increase in difficulty. However, an additional, critical factor in determining the difficulty of a text for English language learners is the familiarity of the vocabulary. Note that:

> There is now a large body of studies indicating that poor readers primarily differ from good readers in context-free word recognition, and not in deficiencies in ability to use context to form predictions.[2]

Learners of English must be able to recognize a great many words on sight so that they can absorb, understand, and react to the text much as they would to a text in their first language.

The *Password* series is distinguished by its meticulous control and recycling of vocabulary so that the readings consistently maintain an appropriate level of difficulty. When learners can recognize enough of the words in their reading materials, they can then develop and apply reading skills and strategies. The result is an authentic reading experience, the kind of experience learners need to become proficient readers of English.

2. An intensive reading program is essential to prepare English language learners for the demands of college and careers.

An intensive reading program means students engage in the careful reading of nonfiction texts with the goal of understanding them in detail, under the guidance of the teacher. A well-designed textbook can play a critical role in helping students not only meet that goal but also acquire reading skills and strategies they can apply to further reading. Course materials should provide practice with the types of thinking skills that students need, not only to comprehend explicitly stated information but to interpret texts, draw inferences, analyze the language, make comparisons, and cite evidence from the text to support their views. The materials should also facilitate collaboration with classmates throughout the process. When their classroom discussions are stimulating and rewarding, students are motivated to do the assigned readings and thus get the reading practice they need.

3. An ELT reading textbook should teach the English vocabulary that will be most useful to learners.

Corpus-based research has shown that the 2,000 highest-frequency words in English (as identified in Michael West's classic *General Service List*) account for about 80 percent of the running words in academic texts.[3] The *New General Service List*, with 2,368 high-frequency "word families," goes even further, providing 90 percent coverage of the words in most general English texts.[4] Clearly, the highest-frequency words are highly valuable words for students of English to learn.

The *Password* target word lists are based on analyses of high-frequency word data from multiple sources, including the Longman Corpus Network. Also taught in the series are common collocations and other multiword units, such as phrasal verbs, while a few target words have been chosen for their value in discussing a particular topic. With the increasing interest in corpus-based research in recent years, a wealth of information is now available as to which words are the highest-frequency, be it in US and/or British academic contexts, in written English of various types, in spoken English, and so on. Teachers may worry about how to choose from among the various lists, but at the level of the 2,000 highest-frequency words in general use—the level of the *Password* series—the lists are far more alike than they are different.

While becoming a good reader in English involves much more than knowing the meanings of words, there is no doubt that vocabulary knowledge is essential. To learn new words, students need to see and understand them repeatedly and in varied contexts. They must also become skilled at guessing the meaning of new words from context, but they can do this successfully only when they understand the context.

Research by Paul Nation and Liu Na suggests that "for successful guessing [of unknown words] . . . at least 95% of the words in the text must be familiar to the reader."[5] For that reason, the vocabulary in the readings has been carefully controlled so that unknown words should constitute no more than five percent of any reading passage. The words used in each reading are limited to those high-frequency words that the learner is assumed to know, or has studied in previous chapters, plus the new vocabulary being taught. New vocabulary is explained and practiced in exercises and activities, encountered again in later chapters, and reviewed in the Unit Checkpoints and Self-Tests. This emphasis on systematic vocabulary acquisition is a highlight of the series.

The chart below shows the number of words that each *Password* book assumes will be familiar to the learner, and the range of the high-frequency vocabulary targeted in the book.

The five books in the series vary somewhat in organization, to meet the diverse needs of beginning to high-intermediate students, as well as in the increasing complexity of the reading materials and exercises. All five books will help learners make steady progress in developing their reading, critical thinking, and vocabulary skills in English. Please see the Overview in each book for detailed information about its organization and contents, including the exciting new features the third edition has to offer.

Linda Butler, creator of the Password *series*

Additional References

Grabe, William. *Reading in a Second Language: Moving from theory to practice.* Cambridge: Cambridge University Press, 2009.

Liu, Dilin. "The Most Frequently Used Spoken American English Idioms: A Corpus Analysis and Its Implications," *TESOL Quarterly* 37 (Winter 2003): 4, 671– 700.

Nation, I.S.P. *Teaching Vocabulary: Strategies and techniques.* Boston: Heinle, Cengage Learning, 2008.

Schmitt, Norbert, and Cheryl Boyd Zimmerman. "Derivative Word Forms: What Do Learners Know?" *TESOL Quarterly* 36 (Summer 2002): 145–171.

[1] Thom Hudson, *Teaching Second Language Reading* (Oxford, UK: Oxford University Press, 2007) 291.
[2] C. Juel, quoted in *Teaching and Researching Reading*, William Grabe and Fredericka Stoller (Harlow, England: Pearson Education, 2002) 73.
[3] I. S. P. Nation, *Learning Vocabulary in Another Language* (Cambridge, England: Cambridge University Press, 2001) 17.
[4] "A New General Service List (1.01)." (n.d.) Retrieved December 15, 2015, from http://www.newgeneralservicelist.org
[5] Nation 254

Highest-frequency words	Password 1	Password 2	Password 3	Password 4	Password 5
2,000					
					target words *absence, acceptable, advantage, . . .*
1,500				**target words** *appear, attach, . . .*	**words assumed** *a/an, able, about, active, address, adult, agree, almost, amount, appear, attach, . . .*
1,200			**target words** *active, amount, . . .*	**words assumed** *a/an, able, about, active, address, adult, agree, almost, amount, . . .*	
900		**target words** *able, adult, . . .*	**words assumed** *a/an, able, about, address, adult, agree, almost, . . .*		
600	**target words** *agree, almost, . . .*	**words assumed** *a/an, about, address, agree, almost, . . .*			
300	**words assumed** *a/an, about, address, . . .*				

OVERVIEW OF *PASSWORD 1*, THIRD EDITION

Password 1 is intended for beginning-level students who need to build a solid foundation for reading in English, whether for academic purposes or for their careers. Each chapter features an engaging nonfiction reading passage as the basis for a variety of activities to help students develop their reading, critical thinking, speaking, writing, and vocabulary skills.

The book assumes students start out with a vocabulary of about 300 words in English, and it teaches over 150 more of the high-frequency words and phrases that students most need to know at this point in their study of English. In each chapter, eight to ten words and phrases are highlighted in the reading passage, taught and practiced in the exercises, and all recycled in later chapters. Additional terms are taught in Tips in the margins and in the Critical Thinking sections. Because of the systematic building of vocabulary, as well as the progression of the skills work, it is best to do the chapters in order.

The target vocabulary consists primarily of words found among the 600 highest-frequency words in English. Occasionally, lower-frequency words and phrases are targeted for their usefulness in discussing a particular theme, as in the unit on friendship, where students will learn *each other*, *trust*, and *tell the truth*.

Organization of the Book

Password 1 contains five units, each with three chapters and a *Checkpoint* chapter. Vocabulary Self-Tests are found after Units 2, 4, and 5. The answers to the Self-Tests and the Index to the Target Vocabulary are at the end of the book.

THE UNITS   Each unit is based on a theme, and each chapter in the unit is built around a reading about a real person, situation, or event.

★ **New in this edition:** Each unit opens with a *Think about This* question, designed to activate prior knowledge of the unit theme. It will get students thinking and talking about the topic from the start.

THE CHAPTERS   Each of the three chapters in a unit is organized as follows:

Getting Ready to Read—The chapter opens with a photo and a pre-reading task. The tasks are for class discussion or pair or small-group work. *Getting Ready to Read* improves students' reading comprehension by activating schema. The tasks get them to connect with the topic before they read by raising questions, eliciting what students already know, asking for their opinions, and introducing key vocabulary.

★ **New in this edition:** The new, color photo will spark interest in the topic. The *Learning Outcome* tells students the content objective of the chapter: what they will be reading, talking, and learning about by working through the chapter.

Reading—This section contains the reading passage for the chapter. The passages progress from about 175 to about 300 words over the course of the book. Students should do the reading the first time without stopping to look up or ask about new words. Careful control of the vocabulary in each passage means that students will not get derailed by too many new words and can have the authentic reading experience they need to build their reading skills.

Audio recordings of the readings are available in the **Essential Online Resources**, for which this book contains an access code inside the front cover. Students can play the audio recording of the passage while they reread it, as listening while reading can aid comprehension, retention, and pronunciation.

Each reading passage is followed by *Quick Comprehension Check*, a brief true/false exercise to help students monitor their general understanding of the passage. At this point, students focus only on comprehension of the major points in the reading. Vocabulary study and an in-depth examination of the text will follow.

★ **New in this edition:** The Reading section now opens with a *Read to Find Out* question, to give students a goal for their reading. Unit 4 has a new theme, friendship, and the readings are new, as are all other materials in the unit. Other readings in the book have been updated for this edition. Also new is part B of the *Quick Comprehension Check*: students must locate and cite evidence from the reading to support their answers and to make corrections to the false statements. These are essential skills for academic reading.

Exploring Vocabulary—This section teaches the target vocabulary from the reading. In *Thinking about the Target Vocabulary*, students complete a list of target words and phrases from the reading, organized in alphabetical order. After they circle those terms that are new to them, students return to the reading to see what they can learn about the words from the context in which they are used. Students can do this vocabulary work independently or in pairs, but they will benefit from doing it first as a whole class, with the teacher's guidance.

Using the Target Vocabulary follows, with four exercises to help students understand the meanings of the target words and phrases as they are used both in the reading and in other contexts. The exercises can be done in class, by students working individually or in pairs, or for homework. After working through the exercises in *Exploring Vocabulary*, students can turn to their dictionaries for further information, if needed.

★ **New in this edition:** *Vocabulary Tips* in the margins teach vocabulary strategies or new terms or provide extra information about the meanings and uses of particular target words and phrases.

Developing Your Reading Skills—Re-reading is a vital part of the reading process, and the tasks in this section motivate students to delve back into the reading passage and thereby deepen their understanding of the text. The tasks include work on identifying topics and main ideas, scanning, recognizing cause and effect relationships, understanding pronoun reference, distinguishing fact from opinion, and summarizing the reading. Developing these skills is essential preparation for academic reading in English.

★ **New in this edition:** Essential skills for academic reading have been added throughout the chapters. New tasks help students use graphic organizers. *Reading Tips* in the margins teach reading strategies and offer advice on good reading habits.

Critical Thinking—This new section for the third edition adds rigor to the discussion of the reading passages by requiring students to analyze and evaluate what the writer is saying before they offer their own opinions and reactions to the reading. Students are guided to examine the text, make inferences, draw comparisons, cite evidence--in short, to apply a range of vital thinking skills and demonstrate a thorough understanding of the text. The section may also include community-building questions, inspired by the readings, that get students to use their imaginations and share their own experiences and ideas.

★ **New in this edition:** Questions for discussion promote the critical thinking skills expected and required for success in college and careers in the 21st century. *Critical Thinking Tips* in the margins help students to develop those skills and become more aware of them.

Writing—Part A, *Use the Target Vocabulary*, gives students tasks for using the target vocabulary in sentences, which students then share with a partner. Part B in Units 1–3 is *Practice Listening and Writing*, a dictation exercise, and Part C is *Writing Practice*, an exercise that requires students to write sentences. For *Writing Practice* in Units 4 and 5, students write a paragraph on a topic related to the reading. These paragraph-writing tasks can be used for brief in-class writing, as prompts for journal entries, or for more formal assignments that may require multiple drafts. Students are encouraged to share their paragraphs, a practice which helps them develop awareness of writing for an audience and gives their partner an additional theme-based reading experience.

★ **New in this edition:** *Writing Tips* in the margins provide strategies to help students become more successful writers.

UNIT CHECKPOINT Each unit ends with a Checkpoint chapter, which is designed to help students review and expand on the content of the unit. The Checkpoint begins with a *Look Back* section, in which students are asked to recall and reflect on what they learned (*Think About This*) and think about their own response to each of the reading passages (*Remember the Readings*). *Reviewing Vocabulary* gives students another point of interaction with the target vocabulary from the unit; students see the vocabulary in new contexts and have the chance to test what words and phrases they remember and can use. *Expanding Vocabulary* teaches students about word families and word parts, and *A Puzzle* puts target vocabulary into a crossword or word search puzzle. The final section, *Extra Reading*, provides another reading passage on the unit theme and recycles target vocabulary from previous readings. It is followed by *Comprehension Check*, two reading skills exercises, and *Critical Thinking*.

★ **New in this edition:** A *Learning Outcome* now introduces each Checkpoint chapter. The new *Look Back* section provides a valuable follow-up to the students' reading experiences in each unit. The new *Critical Thinking* questions provide another opportunity for class discussion of key points in the reading and inferences to be drawn from it.

THE VOCABULARY SELF-TESTS Three multiple-choice vocabulary tests appear in the book, the first covering Units 1 and 2, the second covering Units 3 and 4 , and the third, all five units. The answers are given at the back of the book, as these tests are intended for students' own use so that they can review the target vocabulary and assess their progress.

★ **New in this edition:** The Self-Tests have been updated to include the new target vocabulary.

NEW Essential Online Resources

A new set of resources is available for *Password 1*. It contains:

- Audio recordings of each reading
- Bonus activities for extra practice in timed reading and study skills
- The Teacher's Manual, containing:
  - Notes to the teacher
  - The answer key for all exercises in the book, updated for this edition
  - Five unit tests with answers, updated for this edition (each test containing a theme-based reading passage, reading skills tasks based on the passage, and eight test items on the unit vocabulary)

To the Student

Welcome to *Password 1!* This book will help you read better in English and teach you many new words. I hope you will have fun using it.

ACKNOWLEDGMENTS, CREDITS, AND ABOUT THE AUTHOR

Photo Credits

Front cover: Pairat Pinijkul/Shutterstock; **Page 1:** Jakub Cejpek/123RF; **2 (T):** Wavebreakmedia/Shutterstock; **2 (BL):** TTstudio/Shutterstock; **2 (BC):** Miks Mihails Ignats/Shutterstock; **2 (BR):** Cheryl Casey/Shutterstock; **3:** Courtesy of Mayda Saldana; **9 (T):** Denice Breaux/Getty Images; **9 (BL):** PA Images/Alamy Stock Photo; **9 (BM):** Nancy Kaszerman/ZUMAPRESS.com/Alamy Stock Photo; **9 (BR):** WENN Rights Ltd/Alamy Stock Photo; **10:** Courtesy of Julie Akeret and Will Daniel; **17:** Courtesy of Linda Butler and Daniel Butler; **24:** Jakub Cejpek/123RF; **29:** Rido/Adobe Stock Photo; **30:** Travenian/Getty Images; **37:** Amble Design/Shutterstock; **44 (T):** Lightwavemedia/Shutterstock; **44 (a):** Zone Creative/Adobe Stock Photo; **44 (b):** Levente Gyori/Shutterstock; **44 (c):** Elena Schweitzer/Shutterstock; **44 (d):** Urfin/Shutterstock; **44 (e):** Luis carlos jimenez del rio/123RF; **44 (f):** Marilyn Barbone/Adobe Stock Photo; **44 (g):** Magone/123RF; **52:** Rido/Adobe Stock Photo; **56:** Dmytro Zinkevych/Shutterstock; **61:** Shutterstock; **62:** Africa Studio/Adobe Stock Photo; **69:** Henry Westheim Photography/Alamy Stock Photo; **76 (T):** Isabelle Plasschaert/Alamy Stock Photo; **76 (BL):** Azndc/Getty Images; **76 (BM):** Fesus Robert/Shutterstock; **76 (BR):** Daniel Sambraus/Getty Images; **77:** Timothy A. Clary/AFP/Getty Images; **79 (T):** Cultura/Seb Oliver/Getty Images; **79 (M):** Andrey Popov/Shutterstock; **79 (B):** Golden Pixels LLC/Shutterstock; **84:** Shutterstock; **91:** Shutterstock; **92:** Dragon Images/Shutterstock; **95 (1):** Maria Symchych/Shutterstock; **95 (2):** Drobot Dean/Adobe Stock Photo; **95 (3):** Adobe Stock Photo; **95 (4):** Image Hit/Adobe Stock Photo; **100:** Gareth Boden/Pearson Education Ltd;**108:** Stock Photo Pro/Adobe Stock Photo; **111 (1):** Mukhina1/Getty Images; **111 (2):** Ryasick/Getty Images; **111 (3):** Michaeljung/Shutterstock; **111 (4):** Pakphoto/Adobe Stock Photo; **115:** Shutterstock; **119:** Christopher Pillitz/Getty Images; **125:** AVAVA/Shutterstock; **126:** Moodboard/Adobe Stock Photo; **134:** A_Lesik/Shutterstock; **142:** Fuse/Getty Images; **149:** AVAVA/Shutterstock; **153:** Iofoto/Shutterstock.

Illustration Credits

ElectraGraphics, Inc.

Acknowledgments

I would like to thank Mayda Saldana, Will Daniel, and Daniel Butler for sharing their stories with me for *Password 1*. I would also like to thank my beginning reading students at Holyoke Community College (Holyoke, MA, USA), whose responses to the readings and exercises we used in class helped to shape the book.

I also very much appreciate the work of the following reviewers, who commented on early drafts of materials for the book: Simon Weedon, NOVA ICI Oita School, Japan; Joe Walther, Sookmyung Women's University, Korea; Kevin Knight, Kanda University of International Studies, Japan; Guy Elders, Turkey; Wendy Allison, Seminole Community College, Florida; Kimberly Bayer-Olthoff, Hunter College, New York; Ruth Ann Weinstein, J.E. Burke High School, Massachusetts; Vincent LoSchiavo, P.S. 163, New York; Kelly Roberts-Weibel, Edmunds Community College, Washington; Lisa Cook, Laney College, California; Thomas Leverett, Southern Illinois University, Illinois; Angela Parrino, Hunter College, New York; Adele Camus, George Mason University, Virginia.

Finally, I would like to thank my brilliant development editor, Penny Laporte, and everyone on the Pearson English team for all their efforts on behalf of this book and the entire *Password* series. It has been a pleasure working with you.

About the Author

Linda Butler began her English language teaching career in Italy in 1979. She earned a master's in TESOL at Boston University and has since taught in several college ESL programs in the United States. She writes and edits online and print materials for learning, teaching, and testing English, and she is the author of many ESL/EFL textbooks, including Books 1 through 4 of the *Password* series and *Longman Academic Writing Series 1: Sentences to Paragraphs*.

LEARNING SOMETHING NEW

THINK ABOUT THIS

How do you like to learn to do new things?

Check (✓) your answers, and add your own ideas.

- From family and friends
- From teachers
- From books or magazines
- From TV or the Internet
- Your idea: ______________

CHAPTER 1

Mayda Learns to Swim

In the pool

LEARNING OUTCOME

› Learn about a beginning swimmer

GETTING READY TO READ

Talk about these questions with your class.

1. Do students in your country learn to swim at school?

2. Look at the pictures. Are these good places to swim? Circle Yes or No. Tell why or why not.

In a lake   Yes / No

In a river   Yes / No

In the ocean   Yes / No

READING

Read to Find Out: Does Mayda swim in the ocean?

Look at the words and picture next to the reading. Then read. Do not stop to use a dictionary.

Mayda Learns to Swim

1. Mayda Saldana is from Mexico. Now she is a college student in the United States. **Every** day, she goes to her classes. For one class, she does not have papers or books. This class is not in a classroom. It's in a pool. It's a swimming class.

2. Mayda's class is for **beginners**. Swimming is new for all the students in the class. Mayda says she is **afraid** of the water, and the class is not easy for her. She says, "It's easy for children to learn new things, but I'm not young!"

Mayda

3. Mayda is taking the swimming class **because** she wants to learn to swim. Her sister can swim, and her friends can swim. She wants to go swimming with them. She doesn't want to be afraid. She doesn't like that **feeling**. That is why she **practices** swimming in class, and she goes to the pool for **extra** practice on weekends.

[1] *little by little = slowly*

4. Mayda says, "I'm not very good, but I'm learning, little by little.[1] Being in the pool is OK now. But the ocean? Oh no, I'm not **ready** for that. There are things like sharks[2] in the ocean!"

[2] *a shark*

Quick Comprehension Check

A. Read these sentences **about the reading**. Circle T (true) or F (false). On the line, write the number of the paragraph with the answer.

1. Mayda goes to college in the United States ⓉF   _1_
2. One of her classes is in a swimming pool. T F _____
3. The class is easy for Mayda. T F _____
4. She feels OK in the pool now. T F _____
5. She loves to swim in the ocean. T F _____

B. Work with your class. Share your answers from part A. Go back to the reading to show why a sentence is true or false. Correct the false sentences.

EXPLORING VOCABULARY

Thinking about the Target Vocabulary

A. These words come from "Mayda Learns to Swim" on page 3. They are in *alphabetical* order. Circle the words that are new to you.

1. **a**fraid
2. **bec**ause
3. **beg**inners
4. **ev**ery

5. **ex**tra
6. **f**eeling
7. **p**ractices
8. **r**eady

B. Go back to the reading. Look for the words you circled. What do you think they mean?

Understanding the Target Vocabulary

A. Complete the sentences with the words in the box. The sentences are **about the reading**.

because	beginners	✔ every	extra	feeling

1. Mayda has classes on Monday, Tuesday, Wednesday, Thursday, and Friday. She goes to class _______ every _______ day of the week but not on weekends.

2. Swimming is new for the students in Mayda's class. This is their first time in a swimming class. They are _______________.

3. Why does Mayda go to swimming class? She goes _______________ she wants to learn to swim.

4. Mayda doesn't like being afraid. Being is afraid not a good _______________.

5. Mayda swims in class, but the classes are short. There isn't much time. She goes to the pool on weekends because she wants _______________ practice.

B. Complete the sentences about the pictures. Write *afraid, practicing,* or *ready.*

1. She is ______________.   2. She is ______________.   3. He is ______________
to run.

C. Complete the sentences with the words in the box.

beginner	every	practices	ready

1. Ann goes to bed at 11:00 ________________ night.

2. Paolo is starting to study English. English is new for him. He is a

    ________________.

3. It is time to go to school. I have my books. I am ________________ to go.

4. Tina is a basketball player. She ________________ from 3:00 to 5:00 P.M.

    every day.

D. Complete the sentences with the words in the box.

afraid	because	extra	feelings

1. Robert is not going to class today ________________ he feels sick.

2. There are 10 people but 12 chairs. There are two ________________

    chairs.

3. Some people are ________________ of flying. They do not like

    airplanes.

4. Is Tom happy? I don't know. He doesn't talk about his

    ________________.

> **Writing Tip:**
> Use *afraid + of
> + something* or
> *someone: She's
> afraid of flying.* Use
> *afraid + to + do
> something: She's
> afraid to fly.*

DEVELOPING YOUR READING SKILLS

The Topic and the Main Idea

What's the Topic? What's the Main Idea?

A reading has a **topic** and a **main idea**.

Ask, "What is the reading about?" The answer is the **topic** of the reading.

Ask, "What does the reading say about the topic?" The answer is the **main idea** of the reading.

A. Go back to page 3 and read "Mayda Learns to Swim" again.

B. Answer the questions about the topic and the main idea of the reading.

1. What is "Mayda Learns to Swim" about? Check (✔) the topic.
   - ☐ a. College classes
   - ☐ b. Mayda Saldana
   - ☐ c. Things in the ocean
2. What does the reading say about the topic? Check (✔) the main idea.
   - ☐ a. You can learn to swim at school.
   - ☐ b. Some people are afraid of the water.
   - ☐ c. Mayda Saldana is learning to swim in college.

> **Reading Tip:** You understand more and remember more when you read something again.

Remembering Details

Which sentence is true? Circle *a* or *b*.

1. a. Mayda Saldana goes to college in Mexico.
   b. Mayda Saldana goes to college in the United States.

2. a. Mayda is afraid to go in the water.
   b. Mayda is afraid of her swimming class.

3. a. Mayda says, "It's easy for me to learn new things."
   b. Mayda says, "It's easy for children to learn new things."

4. a. Mayda wants to swim with her sisters and brothers.
   b. Mayda wants to swim with her family and friends.

5. a. Mayda says, "Being in the pool is OK now."
   b. Mayda says, "Being in the ocean is OK now."

> **Reading Tip:** The main idea is the most important idea in a reading. The details help explain the main idea.

Summarizing the Reading

> **What's a Summary?**
>
> A **summary** of a reading tells the main idea and important details in the reading. It is much shorter than the reading. It does not repeat sentences from the reading.

Complete the summary of the reading on page 3. Write *afraid, beginners, learning,* and *practices.*

Mayda Saldana is _____*learning*_____ to swim in college. She is in a
(1)

swimming class for __________________. She is __________________ of the water,
(2) (3)

but that does not stop her. She __________________ in class and on weekends.
(4)

CRITICAL THINKING

Discussion

Talk about these questions with your class.

1. Why does Mayda want to learn to swim? Find two answers to this question in the reading.

2. Mayda is doing two things to learn to swim. What are they?

3. Mayda says, "I'm not young!" Why does she say this? Is it easy for children to learn new things? Are there things that children can learn more easily than adults? Tell what you think and why.

4. Does Mayda feel the same way about the pool and the ocean? Tell why or why not. Do you think she will swim in the ocean? Do you think it's good to do things that you are afraid of? Talk about a time when you did something you were afraid to do.

5. How important is it to know how to swim? Give your answer as a number from 0 to 3:

   3 = It's very important for everyone.

   2 = It's important for many people.

   1 = It's important for some people.

   0 = It's not important.

> **Critical Thinking Tip:** In this book, you will be able to practice critical thinking. Using critical thinking will help you understand more of what you read.

WRITING

A. Use the Target Vocabulary: Complete the sentences. Copy your sentences on a piece of paper. Then find a partner and read your partner's sentences.

1. Many people are **afraid** of ________________________.

2. I need to **practice** ________________________.

3. I want to learn English **because** ________________________.

4. I ________________________ **every** day.

5. I can talk to ________________________ about my **feelings**.

B. Practice Listening and Writing: Get ready for a dictation. Practice writing these sentences. Then close your book. Take a piece of paper. Your teacher will say the sentences. Listen and write the sentences.

1. Go to school.
2. Be ready to learn.
3. Work with your class.
4. Don't be afraid.
5. Find extra time to practice English.

C. Writing Practice: Read the questions. Write your answers on a piece of paper. Write complete sentences. Then find a partner and read your partner's sentences.

1. What is your name?
2. Where are you from?
3. What are you learning?
4. When do you practice English?

Example:

1. My name is Nelson.
2. I am from the Philippines.
3. I am learning English.
4. I practice English every day in class and on weekends at work.

CHAPTER 2

Learning to Make Movies

LEARNING OUTCOME

› Learn about someone who likes making movies

GETTING READY TO READ

Talk about these questions with your class.

1. Look at the photo. What do you see?

2. What are the names of these actors? Who are some actors that you like?

3. Do you, your family, or your friends sometimes make movies? Tell when and how. Do you sometimes put your movies online[1]?

[1] *online* = on the Internet

Read to Find Out: What does Will do in the summer?

Look at the words and picture next to the reading. Then read. Do not stop to use a dictionary.

Learning to Make Movies

1   Will Daniel loves movies. He and his friends like to see new movies. But Will does not **just** watch movies. He is learning to make them, **too**. Read this interview[1] with Will.

2   *Interviewer:*   Will, how are you learning about making movies?

3   *Will:*   At home, I watch a lot of movies online. I watch a lot of interviews with directors,[2] too. You can learn a lot by listening to directors.

4   *Interviewer:*   Do you have a **favorite** director?

5   *Will:*   Yeah, Steven Spielberg. He makes great movies.

6   *Interviewer:*   Can you learn about making movies at your high school?

7   *Will:*   Yes, I'm in a club after school and I'm learning to **use** a movie camera.[3] I make movies with the **other** people in the club. We make short movies, just four or five minutes long.

8   *Interviewer:*   And you go to film[4] school in the summer, don't you?

9   *Will:*   That's right. I learn about acting and directing there, too. We do a little of **everything**—writing, making costumes,[5] using lights. We're **busy** from morning to night. We have classes eight or nine hours a day, and sometimes **more**.

10   *Interviewer:*   That's a lot of work! What about after high school? Do you want to study film in college?

11   *Will:*   I want to study acting, but my mom and dad don't like that idea.

Will Daniel

[1] *an interview* = a conversation with one person asking many questions

[2] *a director* = the person who tells the actors in a movie what to do

[3] *a movie camera*

[4] *film* = movie

[5] *costumes* = clothes for actors in movies

Quick Comprehension Check

A. Read these sentences **about the reading**. Circle T (true) or F (false). On the line, write the number of the paragraph with the answer.

1. Will is learning to make movies.   T   F   _____
2. He watches movies online.   T   F   _____
3. He is a college student.   T   F   _____
4. He makes short movies at home.   T   F   _____
5. He goes to film school in the summer.   T   F   _____

B. Work with your class. Share your answers from part A. Go back to the reading to show why a sentence is true or false. Correct the false sentences.

EXPLORING VOCABULARY

Thinking about the Target Vocabulary

A. Find the words in **bold** in "Learning to Make Movies" on page 10. Write them in the list. Use alphabetical order.

1. _____busy_____   5. _____________
2. _____everything_____   6. _____________
3. _____________   7. _____________
4. _____________   8. _____________

B. Circle the words in the list that are new to you. Then go back to the reading. Look for the words you circled. What do you think they mean?

Understanding the Target Vocabulary

A. Complete the sentences with the words in the box. The sentences are **about the reading**.

busy	everything	just	more	too

1. Many people watch movies and don't think about them much. But Will

   doesn't _________________ watch movies. He studies them.

2. Will watches movies, and he makes movies, _________________.

3. At film school, Will learns all about making movies. He studies every

   part of how you make a movie. He wants to know _________________
   about making movies.

4. Will has many, many things to do at film school. He is _________________
   all day.

5. Sometimes Will is in class for _________________ than nine hours. He is
   there for 10 hours or 11 hours.

B. Complete the sentences about the picture. Write *favorite*, *other*, or *using*.

The woman on the left is _________________ a TV camera. The
                                (1)

_________________ woman has a microphone. She is doing an
        (2)

interview with the man. He is an actor. Many people like him. He is

their _________________ actor.
            (3)

C. Complete the sentences with the words in the box.

busy	favorite	just	other

1. Maria is a student and a mother. She has a job, too. She is a

   _________________ woman.

2. I love weekends. Saturday and Sunday are my _________________ days of
   the week.

3. Max does not talk in class. He _________________ listens.

4. Lucy likes cats, just cats. She does not like _________________ animals.

D. Complete the conversations with the words in the box.

everything	more	too	use

1. A: Can I please _________________ your phone?

   B: OK. Here you go.

2. A: Why do you want a new job?

   B: I need _________________ money.

3. A: Do you have your books? A pen? A pencil? Some paper?

    B: Yes, I have ________________ in my bag. I'm ready to go.

4. A: Will Smith is my favorite actor.

    B: I like him, ________________.

DEVELOPING YOUR READING SKILLS

The Topic and the Main Idea

A. Go back to page 10 and read "Learning to Make Movies" again.

> **Finding the Topic and the Main Idea**
>
> The topic and the main idea are not the same.
>
> To find the topic, ask, "What is the reading about?"
>
> To find the main idea, ask "What does the reading say about the topic?"

B. Answer the questions about the topic and the main idea of the reading.

1. What is "Learning to Make Movies" about? Check (✔) the topic.
    - ☐ a. Actors and directors
    - ☐ b. Film school
    - ☐ c. Will Daniel

2. What does the reading say about the topic? Check (✔) the main idea.
    - ☐ a. Movies are fun to watch.
    - ☐ b. Will Daniel and his friends like to go to the movies.
    - ☐ c. Will Daniel is learning about making movies.

Reading Tip: The title of this reading is "Learning to Make Movies." Sometimes the title of a reading tells you the topic. Sometimes the title tells you the main idea.

Remembering Details

Which answer is correct? Circle *a* or *b*.

1. Will likes going to see new movies with his ________________.
    a. family   b. friends

2. Will learns a lot about movies from interviews with movie ________________.
    a. directors   b. actors

3. Will is learning how to make movies in ________________ .
   a. an online class   b. a club at his high school

4. Will and the other students make movies that are four or five

   ________________ long.
   a. minutes   b. hours

5. Will goes to ________________ in the summer.
   a. high school   b. film school

6. At film school, Will learns about acting, directing, and ________________
   for movies.
   a. paying   b. writing

7. At film school, the students are in class ________________ hours a day.
   a. four or five   b. eight or more

8. Will wants to study acting in ________________.
   a. Hollywood   b. college

Summarizing the Reading

Complete the summary of the reading on page 10. Use *club, everything, film, interviews,* or *movies.*

Will Daniel loves ________________. He is learning to make them. At home,
                        (1)

he watches movies and ________________ with movie directors. At his high
                            (2)

school, he makes movies in a ________________ after school. He goes to
                                  (3)

________________ school in the summer. Will wants to know ________________
      (4)   (5)

about making movies.

CRITICAL THINKING

Discussion

Talk about these questions with your class.

1. How is Will learning about moviemaking? Tell three places where he is learning about moviemaking. What is he learning in each place?

2. One way to learn something new is learning by doing. What do you think the phrase *learning by doing* means? When is Will learning by doing? What about you? Talk about when, where, and how you are learning by doing.

3. What do you think is Will's favorite part of learning about making movies? What does Will say to make you think that?

4. Will says, "My mom and dad don't like that idea." What idea is he talking about? Why do you think his mother and father feel that way? What do *you* want to study? How does your family feel about this?

> **Vocabulary Tip:** A **phrase** is a group of words that work together in a sentence. *Learning by doing* is a phrase, like *thank you.*

> **Critical Thinking Tip:** Sometimes a reading doesn't tell you everything. This reading doesn't tell you what Will's mother and father say. You have to **guess** (try to think of an answer).

WRITING

A. Use the Target Vocabulary: Complete the sentences. Copy your sentences on a piece of paper. Then find a partner and read your partner's sentences.

1. English is a language. Two **other** languages are ________________ and

    ________________.

2. It is easy to **use** a ________________.

3. I like ________________, and my friends do, **too**.

4. I have **just** one ________________.

5. I think ________________ knows **everything** about ________________.

B. Practice Listening and Writing: Get ready for a dictation. Practice writing these sentences. Then close your book. Take a piece of paper. Your teacher will say the sentences. Listen and write the sentences.

1. Call a friend.
2. Talk about movies.
3. Talk about other things, too.
4. Ask a question.
5. Do you have a camera?

C. Writing Practice: On a piece of paper, write five sentences about your favorite people and your favorite things (for example, actors, singers, foods, sports, cars, places). Then find a partner and read your partner's sentences.

Examples:

My favorite colors are blue and green.
My favorite month is September.

CHAPTER 3

Finding Time for Everything

Dan with his guitar, his books, and his laundry

LEARNING OUTCOME

> Learn about someone who has a busy life

GETTING READY TO READ

Talk about these questions with your class.

1. Look at the photo. What can you guess about Dan from the photo?

2. How many hours are you in class every week?

   ☐ 1–5 hours   ☐ 6–10 hours   ☐ 11–20 hours   ☐ more than 20 hours

3. What other things do you do every week? Check (✔) your answers, and add your own ideas.

   Things I NEED to Do

   ☐ work at a job

   ☐ study

   ☐ go food shopping

   ☐ other: ________________

   Things I LIKE to Do

   ☐ go out with friends

   ☐ listen to music

   ☐ go online

   ☐ other: ________________

Read to Find Out: What is Dan learning to do?

Look at the words and pictures next to the reading. Then read. Do not stop to use a dictionary.

Finding Time for Everything

1   Dan Butler is far from home. His family lives in Hong Kong, but he is studying in the United States. This is his first year in college. He is happy to be there, but he is very **tired**. He is not getting **enough** sleep.

2   Dan is not getting enough sleep because he has many things to do. Every day, he goes to classes. After class, he studies for **a few** hours. Then he goes running. On some days, he works as a lifeguard[1] at the college pool. He **has to** find time for other things, too. **For example**, he has to do his laundry.[2]

3   College cannot be all work, all the time! Dan needs time for fun, too. He is meeting many new people, and he likes **spending** time with them.

4   Dan likes music, too. He can play the guitar **well**. He plays the piano and the cello,[3] too. Every night, he makes music with friends. Then they all go to bed late. In the morning, Dan's classes begin **early**. That is why he is tired. "I yawn[4] a lot in class," he says.

5   "I have to study, and I want to have fun," says Dan, "but I need more sleep. What can I do?" Like other college students, he is learning to manage his time,[5] but it is not easy. Dan wants to know, "How can I find time for everything?"

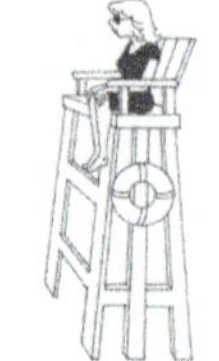

[1] *a lifeguard*

[2] *do his laundry = wash his clothes*

[3] *the piano and the cello*

[4] *He's yawning.*

[5] *manage his time = use his time well*

Quick Comprehension Check

A. Read these sentences **about the reading**. Circle T (true) or F (false). On the line, write the number of the paragraph with the answer.

1. Dan is living at home with his family.   T   F   _____
2. He is busy all day.   T   F   _____
3. He is getting a lot of sleep.   T   F   _____
4. He likes making music with friends.   T   F   _____
5. He is learning to manage his time.   T   F   _____

B. Work with your class. Share your answers from part A. Go back to the reading to show why a sentence is true or false. Correct the false sentences.

EXPLORING VOCABULARY

Thinking about the Target Vocabulary

A. Find the words in **bold** in "Finding Time for Everything" on page 18. Write them in the list. Use alphabetical order.

1. _____*a few*_____

2. _____*early*_____

3. _____________

4. _____________

5. _____________

6. _____________

7. _____________

8. _____________

B. Circle the words in the list that are new to you. Then go back to the reading. Look for the words you circled. What do you think they mean?

Understanding the Target Vocabulary

A. Complete the sentences with the words in the box. The sentences are **about the reading**.

a few	enough	for example	has to	well

1. Dan doesn't feel good. He needs more sleep. He isn't getting

   _____________ sleep.

2. He studies for _____________ hours in the afternoon. He studies for three or four hours.

3. Dan needs to go to class, and he needs to study. He _____________ do these things.

4. He has to do other things, too. _____________, he has to wash his clothes because he needs clean clothes.

5. Dan is a good guitar player. He can play the guitar _____________.

B. Complete the sentences about the pictures. Write *early*, *spending*, or *tired*.

1. She is _____________.

Vocabulary Tip:
Use *spend* with money (*He's spending $100 a week on food*) or time (*I spend an hour on the bus every day*).

2. He is ________________ money.

3. It's ________________ in the morning.

C. Complete the sentences with the words in the box.

early in the morning	enough money	I am tired	well

1. I am going to bed because ____.

2. I have $8, but I need $10. I don't have ________________________________.

3. Joe goes to work at 5:30 A.M. His workday begins ________________

   ____.

4. You're a good singer! You sing very ________________________________.

D. Complete the sentences with the words in the box.

a few	for example	have to	spends

1. I like fruit. ________________, I like oranges, bananas, and apples.

2. There are just ________________ people in the pool—three or four people.

3. Richard studies after class. He ________________ a lot of time on his homework.

4. Children don't want to get shots at the doctor's office,

   but sometimes they ________________ get them.

DEVELOPING YOUR READING SKILLS

The Topic and the Main Idea

A. Go back to page 18 and read "Finding Time for Everything" again.

B. Answer the questions about the topic and the main idea of the reading.

1. What is "Finding Time for Everything" about? Check (✔) the topic.
   - ☐ a. College students
   - ☐ b. Dan Butler at college
   - ☐ c. Finding time for fun

2. What does the reading say about the topic? Check (✔) the main idea.
   - ☐ a. Dan Butler is learning to find time for everything at college.
   - ☐ b. Dan Butler is tired because he has early morning classes.
   - ☐ c. College students have many things to do.

> **Reading Tip:** When you read, don't move your head. Move only your eyes. If your head moves, you may miss words and read more slowly.

Scanning

What Is Scanning?

When you **scan** a reading, you don't read every word. You just look over the reading fast. Use scanning when you go back to a reading to find a word, a number, or an idea.

Scan the reading on page 18. Find the words to complete the sentences.

1. Dan's family is in ________________, but he is in ________________.

2. Every day after class, Dan ________________ for a few hours.

3. Then he goes ________________.

4. Sometimes he works as a ________________ at the college pool.

5. Dan likes music. He can play the ________________, the ________________,

   and the ________________.

6. At night, he plays music with friends and goes to bed ________________.

7. He is learning to manage his ________________.

Summarizing the Reading

A. Match the beginning and the end of each sentence.

_c_   **1.** Dan Butler is

____   **2.** He does not get enough sleep

____   **3.** He needs time for

____   **4.** For example, he likes

____   **5.** He needs to learn

a. because he has to go to class, study, and work.

b. to make music with friends.

c. a tired college student.

d. to use his time well.

e. fun, too.

B. Copy the sentences to complete the summary.

> Dan Butler is a tired college student. He does not get enough sleep...

CRITICAL THINKING

Discussion

Talk about these questions with your class.

1. Dan does some things because he has to. Give four examples from the reading. Dan does other things because he wants to. What are some examples from the reading? Is Dan going to college because he has to or he wants to? How do you know?

2. On page 18, you read that in this chapter, you would learn about "someone who has a busy life." Do you think it's true that Dan has a busy life? Tell why or why not.

3. Find the sentence with an exclamation point (!) in paragraph 3. What does the exclamation point tell you about what the writer thinks? Do you think Dan agrees with the writer? Do you?

4. In paragraph 4, you read that Dan says, "I yawn a lot in class." What does that tell you about Dan? Do you yawn a lot in class? What does your answer say about you?

> **Critical Thinking Tip:**
> Sometimes it's easy to see what the writer thinks about a topic. Someone who thinks the same way **agrees with** the writer. Ask yourself, "Do I agree?"

5. Dan asks, "How can I find time for everything?" What does *everything* mean in this sentence? What can Dan do to manage his time well? Do you think it's easy to manage your time?

WRITING

A. Use the Target Vocabulary: Complete the sentences. Copy your sentences on a piece of paper. Then find a partner and read your partner's sentences.

1. Every day, I **have to** _______________________________ .

2. A teacher **has to** _______________________________ .

3. Some people don't like to _______________ **early** in the morning.

4. Some TV shows are good. **For example**, I like _______________

_______________________________ .

5. I like to **spend** time with _______________________________ .

B. Practice Listening and Writing: Get ready for a dictation. Practice writing these sentences. Then close your book. Take a piece of paper. Your teacher will say the sentences. Listen and write the sentences.

1. Spend time with your friends.
2. Find time to study, too.
3. Use your time well.
4. Do you get enough sleep?
5. Do you go to bed early?

C. Writing Practice: On a piece of paper, write four or more sentences about your weekends. Use *I have to* and *I like to*. Then find a partner and read each other's sentences.

Writing Tip: Write more sentences for extra writing practice. Use *I don't have to* and *I don't like to.*

Examples:

1. On weekends, I have to go to work. I have to do homework, too.
2. On weekends, I like to talk to my sister on the phone. I like to go shopping, too.

Checkpoint

LOOK BACK

A. Think About This

Look back at your answers to the *Think About This* question on page 1:

How do you like to learn to do new things?

Do you want to say anything new?

B. Remember the Readings

What do you want to remember from the readings in Unit 1? For each chapter, write one sentence about the reading.

Chapter 1: Mayda Learns to Swim

____

Chapter 2: Learning to Make Movies

____

Chapter 3: Finding Time for Everything

____

REVIEWING VOCABULARY

Circle the correct word to complete the sentence.

1. Sarah likes cats, but she is _________________ of dogs.
   a. beginner　　　　b. ready　　　　c. afraid

2. Do you have _________________ money, or do you need more?
   a. practice　　　　b. enough　　　　c. favorite

3. Can you _________________ a camera?
   a. use　　　　b. tired　　　　c. spend

4. I don't want to go out _________________ it's very cold.
   a. example　　　　b. because　　　　c. too

5. Please don't eat all the cookies! Take _________________ a few.
   a. more　　　　b. extra　　　　c. just

6. I can't talk on the phone right now. I'm _________________.
   a. other　　　　b. busy　　　　c. early

7. Jack doesn't want to work, but he _________________ to. He needs the money.
   a. well　　　　b. spend　　　　c. has

EXPANDING VOCABULARY

Every

In Chapter 1, you learned the word *every*. In Chapter 2, you learned *everything*. Some other words begin with *every-*, too. Study these words.

everybody or *everyone* = all the people

everywhere = in all the places

Complete the sentences. Use *every*, *everything*, *everyone*, or *everywhere*.

1. The students are ready to begin. _________________ is in the classroom.

2. I know a little about baseball. I don't know _________________.

3. She washes her hair _________________ morning before school.

4. There are flowers _________________ in her house.

5. Does _________________ speak English in the United States?

A PUZZLE

Complete these sentences with words you studied in Chapters 1–3. Look at the word lists on pages 4, 11, and 19 for help. Write the words in the puzzle.

Across

1. I like coffee, and I like tea,
   _too_____________.

4. We need two cups of sugar to make the cookies. Do we have e________________ sugar?

6. Love is a great f_______________.

7. We're waiting for Katya. She isn't r_______________ to go.

8. Six is m________________ than five.

9. To speak English well, you need to p_______________.

11. Tina loves Italian food. For e________________, she loves pizza.

Down

2. I can write with just one hand. I can't write with my o________________ hand.

3. He is starting to learn Spanish. He is a b_______________.

5. I like the Boston Red Sox. Who is your f________________ baseball team?

10. I can't s________________ much money because I don't have much money.

12. There are six chairs but just four people. We have two e________________ chairs.

Learning to Drive

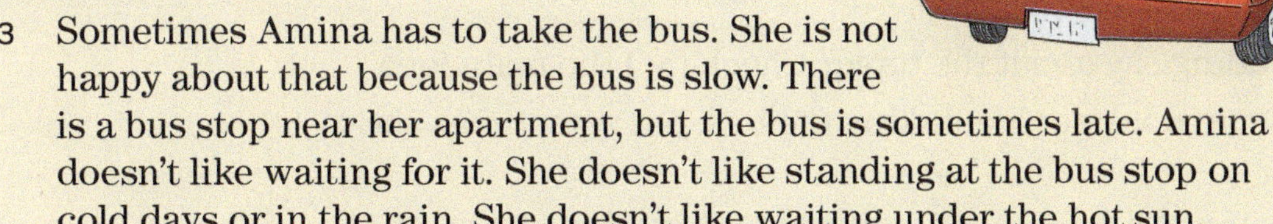

1 Amina Osman is very happy today. She is beginning something new. She is at her first Driver's Ed class. She is learning about driving a car.

2 "Learning to drive will be a good thing for me," says Amina. Now, she has to get rides from her husband, Ali. But Ali works every day. He doesn't always have enough time to give her a ride.

3 Sometimes Amina has to take the bus. She is not happy about that because the bus is slow. There is a bus stop near her apartment, but the bus is sometimes late. Amina doesn't like waiting for it. She doesn't like standing at the bus stop on cold days or in the rain. She doesn't like waiting under the hot sun.

4 Amina is happy about learning to drive, but she is a little afraid, too. The cars on the streets of her city go fast. "I'm going to find quiet streets to practice driving," she says. "My husband is going to help me."

5 Ali is listening to Amina. "I'm ready to help my wife," he says. "But I'm a little afraid, too!"

Comprehension Check

Read these sentences about the reading. Circle T (true) or F (false). On the line, write the number of the paragraph with the answer. Correct the false sentences.

1. Amina is happy about learning to drive.   T   F   _____
2. Her husband can drive a car.   T   F   _____
3. Amina always takes the bus.   T   F   _____
4. She likes the bus.   T   F   _____
5. She is afraid of driving on streets with fast cars.   T   F   _____
6. Ali is going to help Amina learn to drive.   T   F   _____

Scanning

Scan the reading "Learning to Drive." Find the words to complete the sentences.

1. Amina is at her first Driver's Ed ________________.

2. Ali is Amina's ________________.

3. Amina does not like to take the ________________, but sometimes she has to.

4. She does not like waiting at the bus ___________________.

5. She is a little afraid of driving because other cars go ___________________.

6. Ali is ready to teach Amina, but he is a little ___________________.

The Topic and the Main Idea

Answer the questions about the topic and the main idea of the reading.

1. What is "Learning to Drive" about? Check (✔) the topic.

    ☐ a. Buses and cars

    ☐ b. Amina Osman

    ☐ c. A man and his wife

2. What does the reading say about the topic? Check (✔) the main idea.

    ☐ a. Amina Osman does not like taking the bus, but sometimes she has to.

    ☐ b. Amina Osman is happy about learning to drive, but she is afraid, too.

    ☐ c. Amina and her husband, Ali, are learning to drive.

Critical Thinking

Talk about these questions with your class.

1. Paragraph 4 tells us, "Amina is happy about learning to drive, but she is a little afraid, too." Why is she happy? Why is she afraid?

2. How does Ali feel about Amina's learning to drive? How do you know? Why does he feel that way?

3. Do you know how to drive? Tell how you learned to drive or why you don't drive.

I'M HUNGRY! ARE YOU?

THINK ABOUT THIS

How would you answer these questions about food?

Check (✓) your answers.

	Always	Usually	Sometimes	Never
1. Do you like to try new foods?	☐	☐	☐	☐
2. Do you like to shop for food?	☐	☐	☐	☐
3. Do you like to cook?	☐	☐	☐	☐
4. Do you like to read about food?	☐	☐	☐	☐
5. Do you like to talk about food?	☐	☐	☐	☐

CHAPTER 4

The Job of a Food Critic

LEARNING OUTCOME

❯ Learn about what a food critic does

A food critic at work

GETTING READY TO READ

Talk about these questions with your class.

1. When do you eat in restaurants?
   - ☐ every day   ☐ every week   ☐ every month   ☐ never
2. What kinds of restaurants do you like?
   - ☐ Italian restaurants   ☐ fast-food restaurants
   - ☐ Chinese restaurants   ☐ seafood restaurants
   - ☐ Mexican restaurants   ☐ other: _______________

READING

Read to Find Out: What is the job of a food critic?

Look at the words and picture next to the reading. Then read. Do not stop to use a dictionary.

The Job of a Food Critic

1 Do you love food? **Maybe** you **would like** a job as a food critic. Food critics go to restaurants and write about the food. They write for newspapers and websites,[1] for example. The job can be fun, but it's not always easy.

2 First, food critics need to know a lot about food. Some food critics learn by working in restaurant kitchens. Others learn by going to cooking school. All food critics have to read a lot about food.

3 Food critics **also** need to be ready to eat many **kinds** of food. **Most** of the foods will taste[2] good, but some will not. Food critics cannot always go to **the same** restaurants and just eat their favorite things. They have to go to new places, and sometimes they have to eat food they don't like. That part of the job is not fun.

4 Food critics have to be good writers, too. It's not easy to write well about food. Their readers want to know the **details** about the food. For example, how does it look, **smell**, and taste? Their readers want to know about the service,[3] too.

5 Would you like a job as a food critic? Eating and writing about food can be fun, but maybe just eating is more fun.

[1] *a website* = a page or pages on the Internet

[2] *It tastes bad.*

[3] *the service* = the help that workers in the restaurant give you

Quick Comprehension Check

A. Read these sentences **about the reading**. Circle T (true) or F (false). On the line, write the number of the paragraph with the answer.

1. A food critic writes about restaurants and their food.   T   F   ____

2. Food critics work for supermarkets.   T   F   ____

3. Food critics always eat great food.   T   F   ____

4. Food critics have to know a lot about food.   T   F   ____

5. Writing is an important part of a food critic's job.   T   F   ____

B. Work with your class. Share your answers from part A. Go back to the reading to show why a sentence is true or false. Correct the false sentences.

EXPLORING VOCABULARY

Thinking about the Target Vocabulary

A. Find the words in **bold** in "The Job of a Food Critic" on page 31. Write them in the list. Use alphabetical order.

1. _____*also*_____

2. _____________

3. _____________

4. _____________

5. _____________

6. _____________

7. _____________

8. _____________

B. Circle the words in the list that are new to you. Then go back to the reading. Look for the words you circled. What do you think they mean?

Understanding the Target Vocabulary

A. Complete the sentences with the words in the box. The sentences are **about the reading**.

also	details	maybe	most	would like

1. Being a food critic is a good job for some people. _________________ it would be a good job for you. I don't know.

2. Maybe you _________________ to be a food critic. Do you want to be?

3. Food critics go to great restaurants. They _________________ go to restaurants that aren't great.

4. Food critics sometimes have to try foods they don't like, but _________________ of the food they get tastes good. Food critics eat more good food than bad food.

5. A food critic's readers want to know all the _________________ about a restaurant: How does the food look, taste, and smell?

> **Writing Tip:**
> *Also* is like *too* in meaning, but look at these sentences: *Food critics also write a lot = Food critics write a lot, too.* Put *also* before the verb, but use *too* at the end of the sentence.

B. Complete the sentences about the pictures. Write *kinds*, *the same*, or *smells*.

1. The flower _________________ good.

2. Here are five ___________________ of vegetables.

3. These two birds look ___________________.

C. Complete the sentences with the words in the box.

also	details	most	smells

1. What are you cooking? It ___________________ great!

2. A few of the students know a lot of English, but ___________________ of the students are beginners.

3. Greta's first language is German. She can ___________________ speak French and English.

4. John has a new apartment. I don't know how many rooms there are. I don't know any ___________________ about the apartment.

D. Complete the conversations with the words in the box.

kinds	maybe	the same	would like

1. A: Is it going to be a nice weekend?

   B: I don't know. ___________________ it will rain.

2. A: ___________________ you ___________________ something to drink?

   B: Yes, please. I'd like some tea.

3. A: What's your favorite fruit?

   B: I don't have a favorite. I like all ___________________ of fruit.

4. A: Do you go to many movies with Lisa?

   B: Yes, I do because we like ___________________ kind of movies.

> **Vocabulary Tip:**
> Use *would like* (not *want*) and *please* when you ask for something. The short form of *I would* is *I'd*.

DEVELOPING YOUR READING SKILLS

The Topic and the Main Idea

A. Go back to page 31 and read "The Job of a Food Critic" again.

B. Answer the questions about the topic and the main idea of the reading.

1. What is "The Job of a Food Critic" about? Check (✔) the topic.
   - ☐ a. Food
   - ☐ b. Food critics
   - ☐ c. Restaurant jobs
2. What does the reading say about the topic? Check (✔) the main idea.
   - ☐ a. A food critic's job can be fun, but it's not easy.
   - ☐ b. Food critics know a lot of good restaurants.
   - ☐ c. It's easy to get a job as a food critic.

Remembering Details

Which sentence gives a detail from the reading? Circle *a* or *b*.

1. a. Food critics sometimes work for supermarkets.

   b. Food critics sometimes work for newspapers.

2. a. Food critics eat in many restaurants.

   b. Food critics cook in many restaurants.

3. a. A food critic has to know a lot about food.

   b. A food critic has to make a lot of food.

4. a. Food critics always eat their favorite foods.

   b. Food critics can't always eat their favorite foods.

5. a. Food critics have to write well.

   b. Food critics have to write fast.

Summarizing the Reading

Complete the summary of the reading on page 31. Use *also, easy, kinds, know,* or *restaurants.*

Food critics eat in __________________. Then they write about the food,
(1)
usually for a newspaper or website. Food critics have to __________________
(2)
a lot about food. They have to eat many __________________ of food. They
(3)
__________________ have to write well. The job is not __________________, but it
(4)   (5)
can be fun.

CRITICAL THINKING

Discussion

Talk about these questions with your class.

1. How do food critics learn about food? The reading tells three ways. Underline them. What other ways can a person learn about food?

2. The reading says the job of a food critic "can be fun, but it's not always easy" (paragraph 1). Which paragraphs are about the hard parts of the job? What does the writer say are the hard parts of the job? Underline them. Does the job of a food critic seem hard to you? Tell why or why not.

3. Does the writer say anything about spending money in restaurants? What do you think: Who pays for the food when a food critic eats in a restaurant? What makes you think that?

4. Read paragraph 5 again. The first sentence asks, "Would you like a job as a food critic?" Answer the question and tell why or why not. Do you think the writer wants to be a food critic? What makes you think that?

> **Critical Thinking Tip:**
> When a reading tells you what the writer thinks, look for the writer's reasons (why the writer thinks that way). Decide if you do or don't agree with the writer, and what your reasons are.

WRITING

A. Use the Target Vocabulary: Complete the sentences. Copy your sentences on a piece of paper. Then find a partner, and read your partner's sentences.

1. I like many **kinds** of ________________.

2. I always use **the same** ________________.

3. ________________ and ________________ **smell** good.

4. I **would like** ________________.

5. **Maybe** ________________ .

B. Practice Listening and Writing: Get ready for a dictation. Practice writing these sentences. Then close your book. Take a piece of paper. Your teacher will say the sentences. Listen and write the sentences.

1. Many people love good food.
2. Some people like restaurants.
3. Do you like many kinds of food?
4. Would you like to go out to eat?

C. Writing Practice: Think of a restaurant you like. Answer these questions about it. Write your answers on a piece of paper. Then find a partner, and read your partner's sentences.

1. What is the name of the restaurant?
2. Where is it?
3. What kind of food does it have?
4. When do you go there?

Examples:

1. The name of the restaurant is Pintu's.
2. It's in West Springfield.
3. It has Indian food.
4. Sometimes I go there on Friday night.

CHAPTER 5

Who Likes Cereal?

Her favorite snack

LEARNING OUTCOME

❯ Learn about a breakfast food that's not just for breakfast

GETTING READY TO READ

Talk about these questions with your class.

1. Look at the photo. What do you see?

2. What kinds of cereal can you name?

3. Do many people in your country eat cereal?

4. Who do you know that eats cereal? What time of day do they eat it?

Read to Find Out: Who eats cereal in the United States?

Look at the words next to the reading. Then read. Do not stop to use a dictionary.

Who Likes Cereal?

1   Some people say "**breakfast** cereal." Some say "cold cereal." Most people just say "cereal." They are all talking about the same thing. They are talking about an important food in the United States.

2   You can find cereal in every U.S. supermarket. You **may** find 200 kinds of it! Some of them have a lot of sugar or artificial[1] colors, but some kinds are good for you. More than 90 percent[2] of people in the United States—both young and old—say that they like cereal. They buy a lot of it. They buy more than two billion[3] **boxes** of cereal a year. They spend a lot of money on it, too. They spend more on cereal than on bread or hamburgers.

3   In the United States, many people eat cereal at home every morning, but cereal is not just for breakfast. Children can buy cereal for **lunch** at school. Many college students eat it as a **snack**. They eat it at all hours of the day and night. A few colleges have cereal cafés[4] for their students. At these cafés, cereal is all there is.

4   Some people eat cereal for supper,[5] too. They may be tired when they come home from work. They may not want to take the time to cook. A **bowl** of cereal with milk is a **quick** and easy **meal**. Some people do not wait for the bowl or the milk. They just eat their cereal out of the box.

[1] *artificial* = not natural; made by people

[2] *percent* = %

[3] *two billion* = 2,000,000,000

[4] *a café* = a small restaurant

[5] *supper* = a meal eaten in the evening

Quick Comprehension Check

A. Read these sentences **about the reading**. Circle T (true) or F (false). On the line, write the number of the paragraph with the answer.

1. "Breakfast cereal" and "cold cereal" are two names for the same thing.   T   F   _____

2. All supermarkets in the United States have cereal.   T   F   _____

3. People in the United States eat cereal just in the morning for breakfast.   T   F   _____

4. A few college students like cereal, but not many.   T   F   _____

5. Many people, young and old, eat cereal in the United States.   T   F   _____

B. Work with your class. Share your answers from part A. Go back to the reading to show why a sentence is true or false. Correct the false sentences.

EXPLORING VOCABULARY

Thinking about the Target Vocabulary

A. Find the words in **bold** in "Who Likes Cereal?" on page 38. Write them in the list. Use alphabetical order.

1. _____*bowl*_____   5. _____________

2. _____________   6. _____________

3. _____________   7. _____________

4. _____________   8. _____________

B. Circle the words in the list that are new to you. Then go back to the reading. Look for the words you circled. What do you think they mean?

Understanding the Target Vocabulary

A. Complete the sentences with the words in the box. The sentences are **about the reading**.

lunch	may	meals	quick	snack

1. At a U.S. supermarket, you _______________ find just a few kinds

   of cereal, or maybe there will be 200 kinds!

2. Many children eat breakfast at home before school. Later, they eat

   _______________ at school in the late morning or at 12:00 or 12:30 P.M.

3. Sometimes you don't want to eat a lot of food. You want just a

   _______________, like a small bowl of cereal.

4. You don't need a lot of time for cereal. It's _______________ and easy to eat.

5. Some people eat just three times a day: breakfast, lunch, and dinner (or

   supper). Others eat these three _______________ and snacks, too.

> **Writing Tip:** You can use *may* or *maybe* to say the same thing: *I may buy some cereal = Maybe I will buy some cereal.*

B. Complete the sentences about the picture. Write *bowl, box,* or *breakfast.*

The man in the picture is having

_________________. There is a
(1)

_________________ of fruit on the table.
(2)

There is a _______________ of cereal
(3)

next to the fruit.

C. Match the words and their meanings. Write the letters.

_____ 1. meal   a. the first meal of the day

_____ 2. breakfast   b. food and drink that you have at one time

_____ 3. snack   c. a meal eaten in the middle of the day

_____ 4. lunch   d. something small to eat between meals

Vocabulary Tip: In exercise C, a, b, c, and d are **definitions**. A definition is a phrase or sentence that gives the meaning of a word. Look for definitions in your dictionary.

D. Complete the conversations with the words in the box.

bowl	box	may	quick

1. A: What's in this _______________?

    B: My new computer.

2. A: Will you put some water in the cat's _______________?

    B: OK.

3. A: Are you going to see your sister?

    B: Yes, but it'll be just a _______________ visit—maybe
        15 minutes.

4. A: Is it raining?

    B: Not right now, but it _______________ rain later.

Vocabulary Tip: *May* and *might* have the same meaning. Use *may/might* + the base form of a verb: *He's not in class today. He may be (or might be) sick.*

DEVELOPING YOUR READING SKILLS

The Topic and the Main Idea

A. Go back to page 38 and read "Who Likes Cereal?" again.

B. Answer the questions about the topic and the main idea of the reading.

1. What is "Who Likes Cereal?" about? Check (✔) the topic.

   ☐ a. Good breakfasts for children

   ☐ b. Favorite foods in the United States

   ☐ c. Cereal in the United States

2. One sentence gives the main idea of the reading. The other three sentences give details from the reading. Write *main idea* or *detail* on the line.

   _____________ a. Some U.S. supermarkets have 200 kinds of cereal.

   _____________ b. Some children get cereal at school for their lunch.

   _____________ c. Cereal is an important food in the United States.

   _____________ d. Some people eat their cereal out of the box.

> **Critical Thinking Tip:** Read all the answers to a question before you decide which one is correct.

Remembering Details

Which sentence gives a detail from the reading? Circle *a* or *b*.

1. a. Cereal, cold cereal, and breakfast cereal are three kinds of food.

   b. *Cereal, cold cereal,* and *breakfast* cereal are three names for the same thing.

2. a. You can find cereal in most U.S. supermarkets.

   b. You can find cereal in every U.S. supermarket.

3. a. Everyone in the United States eats cereal for breakfast.

   b. Most people in the United States say they like cereal.

4. a. People in the United States buy more than two billion boxes of cereal a year.

   b. People in the United States eat more than two billion bowls of cereal a year.

5. a. They spend more money on cereal than on bread.

   b. They spend more money on cereal than on milk.

6. a. Many U.S. college students love cereal for snacks.

   b. Every U.S. college has a cereal café.

7. a. A cereal café is a small restaurant with a few kinds of food.

   b. A cereal café is a small restaurant with just cereal.

8. a. Most people eat cereal out of the box with no milk.

   b. Some people eat cereal out of the box with no milk.

Summarizing the Reading

A. Match the beginning and the end of each sentence. Write the letters.

____	1. Most people in the United States	a.	just for breakfast.
____	2. Every U.S. supermarket	b.	for snacks, too.
____	3. People young and old eat it, and not	c.	like cereal.
____	4. They may eat cereal at	d.	has many kinds of it.
____	5. They like it	e.	any meal of the day.

B. Copy the sentences to complete the summary. Write them in the form of a paragraph.

> Most people in the United States like cereal.
> Every U.S. supermarket . . .

CRITICAL THINKING

Discussion

Talk about these questions with your class.

1. Who eats cereal in the United States? In paragraphs 2 and 3, underline all the words for the kinds of people the reading tells you about in these two paragraphs. In your country, do all these people eat cereal, too?

2. This circle graph shows something from the reading. What is a good title for this graph? Check (✓) your answer.

   ☐ a. U.S. Children Who Eat Cereal for Breakfast

   ☐ b. U.S. Supermarkets That Sell Cereal

   ☐ c. People in the U.S. Who Like Cereal

> **Critical Thinking Tip:** A **circle graph** (or **pie chart**) can show how something is divided into parts and how big the parts are.

3. Find the answers in the reading: Where do people in the United States eat cereal? Name three places. When do they eat cereal? Complete this sentence telling when and where people in the United States eat cereal: *People in the United States eat cereal . . . .*

4. In paragraph 2, the writer says "Some of them have a lot of sugar or artificial colors." What does "them" mean in this sentence? What does the writer think about eating a lot of sugar and artificial colors? How do you know?

5. What do you think: Is cereal a good breakfast? Is it a good lunch? Is it a good snack? Tell why or why not.

6. In paragraph 4, the reading says, "They just eat their cereal out of the box." Who are "they" in this sentence? Why do they eat their cereal this way? What do you think: Is eating cereal out of the box a good supper?

WRITING

A. Use the Target Vocabulary: Complete the sentences. Copy your sentences on a piece of paper. Then find a partner, and read your partner's sentences.

1. When I want a **snack**, I eat ___________________ or ___________________.

2. I eat ___________________ in a **bowl**.

3. My favorite thing for **lunch** is ___________________.

4. A **quick** and easy meal for me is ___________________.

5. **Most** of my friends ___________________.

B. Practice Listening and Writing: Get ready for a dictation. Practice writing these sentences. Then close your book. Take a piece of paper. Your teacher will say the sentences. Listen and write the sentences.

1. I eat breakfast every day.
2. Do you have lunch at school?
3. I like a snack in the afternoon.
4. What is your favorite meal of the day?

C. Writing Practice: Write your answers to these questions on a piece of paper. Then find a partner, and read your partner's sentences.

1. What is your favorite meal of the day?
2. Where and when do you like to have it?
3. What do you like to eat for this meal?

Examples:

1. My favorite meal of the day is breakfast.
2. I have my breakfast at home at 7:30 a.m.
3. Most days, I have orange juice, coffee, and toast with strawberry jam.

CHAPTER 6

Healthy Eating

LEARNING OUTCOME

❯ Learn about a plan for healthy eating

GETTING READY TO READ

Talk about these questions with a partner.

1. Can you match these words with their pictures? Write *beans, fruit, grains, meat, milk, oil,* and *vegetables*.

a. —————————— b. —————————— c. —————————— d. ——————————

e. —————————— f. —————————— g. ——————————

2. Look at the food in the pictures. Which kinds do you eat every day?

3. The title of this chapter is "Healthy Eating." What does that mean to you?

Read to Find Out: What do the MyPlate guidelines say?

Look at the words and pictures next to the reading. Then read. Do not stop to use a dictionary.

Healthy Eating

1 Children have to eat well to **grow**. We *all* have to eat well to feel good. "Eating well" means eating the right kinds of food. It also means eating the right amounts[1] of food. How do we know what the right kinds are? And the right amounts? The MyPlate guidelines[2] give some answers.

2 This MyPlate picture **shows** a **plan** for eating well. There are five food **groups** in the picture: fruits, vegetables, protein, grains, and dairy. The idea is to eat food from all these food groups every day.

3 There are **different** kinds of food in each group. For example, the dairy group includes[3] milk, cheese, and yogurt. The protein group includes fish, eggs, beans, meat, and nuts. The grains group includes rice, wheat,[4] and corn. It also includes bread, cereal, and tortillas. They're all made from grains.

4 The five parts of the picture are different **sizes**. For example, the part for vegetables is big. The guidelines say men and women need two to three cups of vegetables a day. We don't need as much fruit, so the part for fruit is smaller.

5 Our bodies also need oil. The guidelines say small children need three teaspoons of oil a day. Young men need about seven. Other people need four to six teaspoons. We can get healthy oil from olives[5] and some kinds of beans. (They're in the vegetable group.) We can also get it from fish and nuts. (They're in the protein group.)

6 Most people in the United States know something about healthy eating. They get **information** about it on TV and online. They also hear about it from their doctors. Children learn about healthy eating in school. But do most people **really** eat this way? What do you think?

[1] *amount* = how much (a little or a lot)

[2] *the MyPlate guidelines* = information from the U.S. Department of Agriculture to help people eat well

[3] *includes* = has something in it as a part

[4] *wheat*

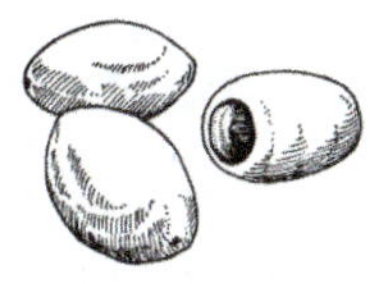
[5] *olives*

Quick Comprehension Check

A. Read these sentences **about the reading**. Circle T (true) or F (false). On the line, write the number of the paragraph with the answer.

1. The MyPlate guidelines tell people what foods are good for you.   T   F _____

2. The MyPlate picture shows six food groups.   T   F _____

3. Meat and milk are in one food group.   T   F _____

4. The guidelines say to eat more fruit than vegetables.   T   F _____

5. The MyPlate picture shows what to eat at every meal.   T   F _____

B. Work with your class. Share your answers from part A. Go back to the reading to show why a sentence is true or false. Correct the false sentences.

EXPLORING VOCABULARY

Thinking about the Target Vocabulary

A. Find the words in **bold** in "Healthy Eating" on page 45. Write them in the list. Use alphabetical order.

1. _different_
2. _______________
3. _______________
4. _______________
5. _______________
6. _______________
7. _______________
8. _______________

B. Circle the words in the list that are new to you. Then go back to the reading. Look for the words you circled. What do you think they mean?

Understanding the Target Vocabulary

A. Complete the sentences with the words in the box. The sentences are **about the reading**.

group	information	plan	really	size

1. MyPlate is a _________________ for eating well. It tells people a good way to eat.

2. A food _________________ has more than one kind of food in it. For example, the dairy group has milk, yogurt, and cheese in it.

Vocabulary Tip: Use *group* for people (*a group of friends*) or for things (*a group of pictures*).

3. The five parts of the MyPlate picture are not all the same ___________________.
   Some are bigger than others.

4. Children learn about healthy eating in school. They get ___________________
   about it from their teachers.

5. Is it true that people in the United States eat this way? Or do they

   ___________________ do something different?

B. Complete the sentences about the pictures. Write *different*, *grow*, or *shows*.

1. Young children ___________________ quickly.

2. These nuts are all ___________________.

3. This map ___________________ where to go.

C. Complete the sentences with the words in the box.

different	groups	grow	size

1. Does your hair ___________________ fast?

2. Flowers don't all smell the same. They have ___________________ smells.

3. She has small feet. What ___________________ shoes does she wear?

4. Sometimes the students work with a partner, and sometimes they work in

   ___________________ of three or four.

D. Complete the conversations with the words in the box.

information	plans	really	show

1. **A:** John says he is 21 years old.

   B: I know, but it's not true. He's ________________ 19.

2. **A:** What do you know about healthy oils?

   B: Not much, but we can find some ________________ online.

3. **A:** What do you think of the ________________ for the new school?

   B: I don't know enough about them. I need more details.

4. **A:** Is that a book about Japan?

   B: Yes, the photos ________________ some beautiful places I want to visit.

DEVELOPING YOUR READING SKILLS

Scanning

Scan the reading on page 45. Find the words to complete the sentences.

1. Children have to eat well to ________________.

2. The picture of the ________________ plan has five parts.

3. These parts are for different food ________________.

4. The biggest part is for ________________.

5. Fish, eggs, and beans are in the ________________ group.

6. Rice and wheat are two kinds of ________________.

7. Two examples of things made from grains are ________________ and

   ________________.

8. Children learn about healthy eating ________________.

Reading Tip: When you read, or when you scan a reading, don't say the words (not even in your head), and don't move your lips. That will slow you down.

Pronoun Reference

What do the **boldfaced** pronouns mean in these sentences? Look back at the reading on page 45. Write the answers.

1. Paragraph 1: **It** also means eating the right amounts of food. _Eating well_

2. Paragraph 1: **We** *all* have to eat well to feel good. _______________

3. Paragraph 5: **They**'re in the vegetable group. _______________

4. Paragraph 5: **They**'re in the protein group. _______________

5. Paragraph 6: **They** also hear about it from their doctors. _______________

Summarizing the Reading

A. Match the beginning and the end of each sentence. Write the letters.

_____ 1. People have to eat well   a. a plan for eating well.

_____ 2. The MyPlate plan is   b. to eat of the different kinds of food.

_____ 3. The MyPlate picture shows five   c. to feel good.

_____ 4. It shows how much   d. get information about healthy eating.

_____ 5. In the United States, it's easy to   e. different food groups.

B. Copy the sentences to complete the summary.

People have to eat well to feel good. The MyPlate plan is

CRITICAL THINKING

Discussion

Talk about these questions in a small group.

1. What does "eating well" mean? Underline the answer the reading gives. What other phrase can you find in the reading that means the same thing as "eating well?" Does the reading say anything about liking the food you eat? Do you think that is also a part of eating well? Give your opinion.

2. Complete the chart with the names of the five food groups. Under the name of each group, write all the examples of foods in each group that you find in the reading. Then write more examples. Have four or more examples for each food group. Use examples that everyone in your group knows.

<table>
<tr><td><u>GROUPS</u></td><td>fruits</td><td></td><td></td><td></td><td></td></tr>
<tr><td>EXAMPLES</td><td></td><td></td><td></td><td></td><td></td></tr>
</table>

3. What do the MyPlate guidelines say about the amount of vegetables that men and women need in a day? Using that information and looking at the picture next to paragraph 2, guess how much fruit men and women need. How many people in your group eat those amounts of fruit and vegetables every day?

4. As a group, make a list of five foods (or more) that the reading doesn't talk about. What do you think the MyPlate guidelines would say about those foods? Why?

5. Reread the questions at the end of paragraph 6. What answer would you give? What makes you think that?

> **Critical Thinking Tip:**
> Some questions (1 and 5, for example) ask for your **opinion**. They ask, 'What do you think?" When you give your opinion, tell why you think that way.

WRITING

A. Use the Target Vocabulary: Complete the sentences. Copy your sentences on a piece of paper. Then find a partner, and read your partner's sentences.

1. I like many **different** kinds of _______________________________.

2. I can **show** you a picture of _______________________________.

3. I would like some **information** about _______________ because

    _______________________________.

4. People sometimes buy _______________ when they do not **really** need to.

5. I have **plans** for _______________________________.

B. Practice Listening and Writing: Get ready for a dictation. Practice writing these sentences. Then close your book. Take a piece of paper. Your teacher will say the sentences. Listen and write the sentences.

1. It is important to eat well.
2. Eat different kinds of food every day.
3. I would like some information, please.
4. These shoes are not the right size.

C. Writing Practice: On a piece of paper, write the names of three or four food groups. Write sentences about foods in these groups that you like and do not like. Then find a partner, and read your partner's sentences.

Food group:_______________

I like _______________ and _______________.

I don't like _______________ or _______________.

Example:

> 1. Food group: fruit
>   I like oranges and blueberries.
>   I don't like grapefruit or bananas.

> **Writing Tip:** Use *and* to connect two things: *He eats fish and chicken.* Change *and* to *or* when the verb is negative: *He doesn't eat beef or pork.*

Checkpoint

LEARNING OUTCOME
> Review and expand on the content of Unit 2

LOOK BACK

A. Think About This

Look back at your answers to the *Think About This* questions about food on page 29. Do you want to say anything new?

B. Remember the Readings

What do you want to remember from the readings in Unit 2? For each chapter, write one sentence about the reading.

Chapter 4: The Job of a Food Critic

____

Chapter 5: Who Likes Cereal?

____

Chapter 6: Healthy Eating

____

REVIEWING VOCABULARY

Circle the correct word to complete the sentence.

1. Many ________________ of fruit and vegetables grow in California.

    a. kinds   b. plans   c. details

2. I eat the ________________ thing for lunch every day: pizza.

    a. most   b. size   c. same

3. I ________________ a cup of tea, please.

    a. show   b. would like   c. grow

4. I'm not very hungry. I don't want a big ________________.

    a. meal   b. may   c. plan

5. There is a big ________________ of apples on the table.

    a. bowl   b. information   c. smell

6. It's important to start the day with a good ________________.

    a. different   b. breakfast   c. box

7. I would like to buy these shoes, but I don't ________________ need them.

    a. snack   b. group   c. really

8. ________________ it will rain. I don't know.

    a. Also   b. Maybe   c. Quick

EXPANDING VOCABULARY

The Suffix -er

Sometimes you can add -er to the end of a word. It changes the word's meaning. Here are three examples. The words ending in -er all mean "a person who (does something)."

   teach + -er = teacher, a person who teaches

   write + -er = writer, a person who writes (Look at the spelling: just one e.)

   swim + -er = swimmer, a person who swims (Look at the spelling: mm.)

A. Look at these words. Take away the -er (or just the -r). Complete the sentence with the new word.

   1. hitter   He can ______*hit*______ a baseball very well.

   2. rider   Can you ______*ride*______ a bicycle?

   3. user   Do you ________________ your right hand or your left when you write?

4. shopper   Where do you _________________ for clothes?

5. dancer   She loves to _________________.

6. planner   He likes to _________________ parties.

B. Add *-er* (or just the *-r*) to the words in the box. Use the new words to complete the sentences.

begin	grow	read	work
drive	play	sing	write

1. She works for a newspaper. She is a ______*writer*______.

2. His sport is volleyball. He is a volleyball _________________.

3. She drives well. She is a good _________________.

4. He is just beginning to study English. He is a _________________.

5. He does his job well. He works hard. He is a good _________________.

6. He grows oranges. He has 3,000 orange trees in California. He is a

   _________________.

7. I like to read, but I am not a fast _________________.

8. Listen to this music! It's by a new group from Brazil. They have a great

   lead _________________.

A PUZZLE

Complete these sentences with words you studied in Chapters 4–6. Look at the word lists on pages 32, 39, and 46 for help. Write the words in the puzzle.

Across

3. What s_______________ box do you need for the books?

4. My new school is d_______________ from my old school.

5. Jack is studying Spanish. He is a_______________ studying Chinese.

6. It m_______________ rain, but I don't think it will.

7. I'm hungry. I think I'll have a s_______________.

8. What are you cooking? It s_______________ great!

Down

1. We may have dinner at home, or _maybe_______________ we will go out to eat.

2. W_______________ you like a drink?

3. This map s_______________ all the streets in the city.

4. I don't know every d_______________ of the plan, just the main parts of it.

6. Do you eat three m_______________ a day?

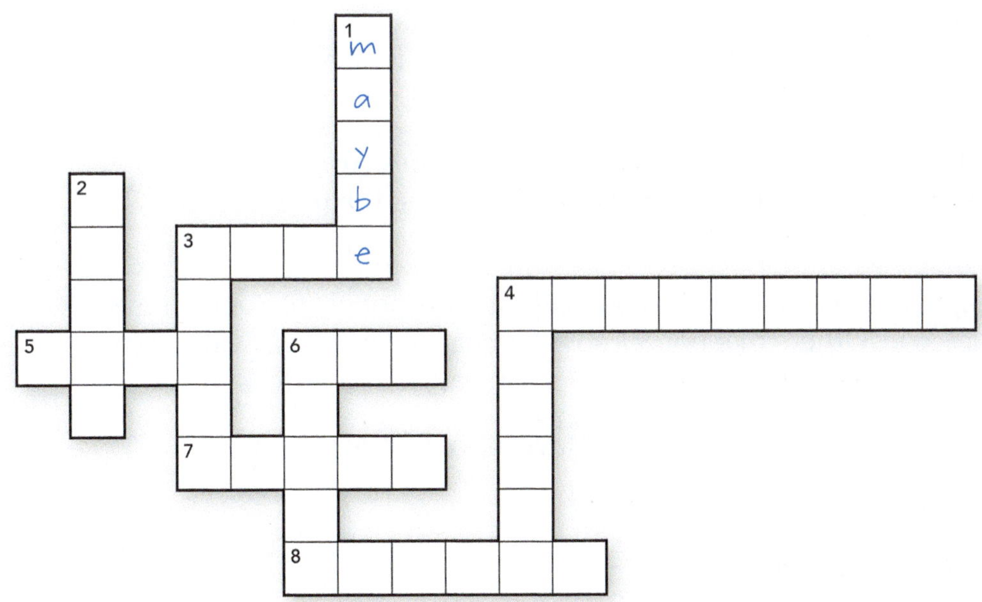

Popcorn

1 Do you like popcorn? Most people in the United States do. Every year, they eat more than 200 cups of it per person.[1] That is a lot of popcorn!

2 Most of the time, they eat it for a snack at home, but they get popcorn in other places, too. They buy boxes of it at baseball or basketball games. They also get it at the movies. Many U.S. movie theaters[2] smell like popcorn.

3 Popcorn is easy to make. All you need are some popcorn kernels[3] and some hot oil. The hot oil makes the kernels pop. That is because every kernel has a little water in it. When the water gets hot, steam[4] makes the kernel pop.

4 Popcorn kernels come in different sizes and colors. You can buy white, yellow, red, purple, or black kernels. After it pops, the popcorn is always white.

5 Many people in the United States put salt on their popcorn. Some like it with butter, too. Others like popcorn with sugar on it. A lot of salt, butter, or sugar is not healthy, but most U.S. doctors say that a little is fine.

6 Would you like a good quick snack? Have a bowl of popcorn!

[1] *per person* = for every person

[2] *a movie theater* = a building where you can see a film

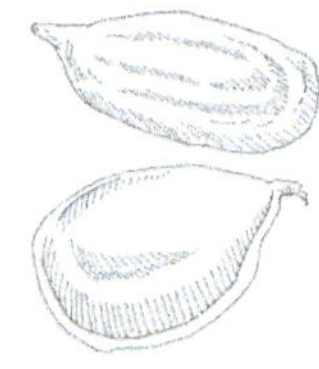

[3] *popcorn kernels*

[4] *steam*

Comprehension Check

Read these sentences about the reading. Circle T (true) or F (false). On the line, write the number of the paragraph with the answer. Correct the false sentences.

1. People in the United States eat a lot of popcorn.   T   F   _____

2. It takes a long time to make a bowl of popcorn.   T   F   _____

3. The water in popcorn makes it pop when it gets hot.   T   F   _____

4. All popcorn is white or yellow.   T   F   _____

5. People in the United States eat popcorn with most meals.   T   F   _____

Scanning

Scan the reading "Popcorn." Find the words to complete the sentences.

1. Every year, people in the United States eat more than _________________ of popcorn per person.

2. Most people in the United States eat popcorn at _________________.

3. Many U.S. _________________ smell like popcorn.

4. People cook popcorn in hot _________________.

5. You can buy popcorn kernels of different _________________ and

   _________________.

6. People sometimes put _________________, _________________, or

   _________________ on popcorn.

The Main Idea of the Reading

One sentence gives the main idea of the reading. The other three sentences give details from the reading. Write *main idea* or *detail* on the line.

_________________ 1. Some people put sugar on their popcorn.

_________________ 2. Many people like to eat popcorn when they watch a movie.

_________________ 3. Most people eat popcorn out of a box or a bowl.

_________________ 4. Many people in the United States like popcorn as a snack.

Critical Thinking

Talk about these questions with your class.

1. Do people in your country eat popcorn? Do they eat it in the same places the reading talks about in paragraph 2? Do they eat it in the same ways the reading talks about in paragraph 5?

2. Do you think popcorn is a healthy snack? Tell why or why not. What is the writer's opinion? How do you know?

3. Why did the writer write "Popcorn"? Check (✔) your answer.

   ☐ a. to tell readers a story about his favorite food

   ☐ b. to talk about a snack that people in the United States love

   ☐ c. to explain why popcorn is a healthy snack

   Which answer did you check? Why?

Vocabulary Self-Test 1

Choose an answer to complete each sentence. Circle the letter of your answer.

Example:

Breakfast is my favorite ______________ of the day.

a. box (b.) meal c. lunch

1. To learn to speak a new language, you have to ______________.
   a. grow b. smell c. practice

2. These shoes are very big. They aren't the right ______________ for me.
   a. bowl b. size c. plan

3. I'd like a pizza with ______________ cheese, please. I love cheese!
   a. early b. tired c. extra

4. There are buses in ______________ cities.
   a. most b. everything c. really

5. The children eat a ______________ after school.
   a. beginner b. snack c. group

6. I'm hungry for some fruit. I ______________ an apple.
   a. for example b. would like c. has to

7. Please put your paper here, with the ______________ papers.
   a. other b. afraid c. also

8. I like chocolate ice cream, and she does, ______________.
   a. because b. too c. favorite

9. Can you ______________ me how to do it?
   a. spend b. show c. quick

10. I know a little Russian, but I can't speak it ______________.
    a. information b. maybe c. well

11. She has a lot to do on weekends. She's always _____________.

    a. different   b. busy   c. every

12. You don't have to pay much for the bus. It's _____________ a dollar.

    a. enough   b. the same   c. just

13. He isn't here now, but he _____________ come later.

    a. may   b. use   c. feeling

14. I have _____________ good friends, not many.

    a. more   b. a few   c. ready

15. Tell me more! I want all the _____________.

    a. kinds   b. details   c. breakfasts

See the Answer Key on page 159.

HAVING FUN

THINK ABOUT THIS

What do you like to do for fun?

Check (✓) your answers, and add your own ideas.

- ☐ Play games
- ☐ Play sports
- ☐ Go shopping
- ☐ Your idea:
- ☐ Listen to music
- ☐ Watch TV or movies
- ☐ Go online

CHAPTER 7

An Easy Game

LEARNING OUTCOME

> Learn about a game played all around the world

Playing Rock, Paper, Scissors

GETTING READY TO READ

Talk about these questions with your class.

1. Which of these games are for children? Which games are for older people? Which games are for everyone?

Hopscotch

Bingo

Cards

Chess

Dominoes

2. Which of the five games do you know how to play? Which is the most fun?

Read to Find Out: How do you play the game Rock, Paper, Scissors?

Look at the pictures and the words next to the reading. Then read. Do not stop to use a dictionary.

An Easy Game

1. Do you know the game Rock, Paper, Scissors? That is what the game is called in the United States, but maybe you know it by a different name. People call it Ching Chong Cha in South Africa. They call it Ca-Chi-Pun in Chile. In Korea, it is called Kawi Bawi Bo. People young and old play this game in countries all **around** the **world**. It's an easy game to play because it has just a few **rules**.

2. There are usually two players in the game, and they usually play the game **standing**. **Each** player **holds** one hand closed. First, the players move their arms up and down, saying "One, two, three!" Then each player makes one of three hand gestures.[1] They have to make the gestures at the same time.

3. The three gestures are Rock, Paper, and Scissors. They look like this.

[1] *gestures =* hand or head movements that mean something

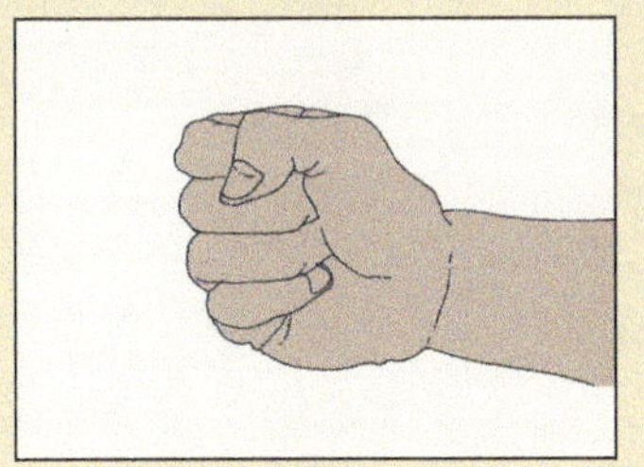
Rock

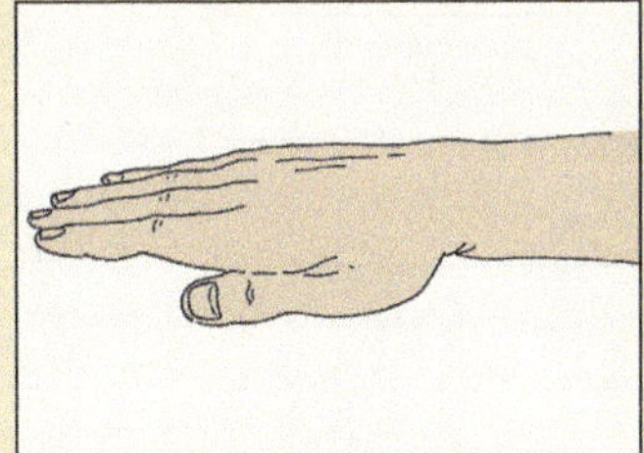
Paper

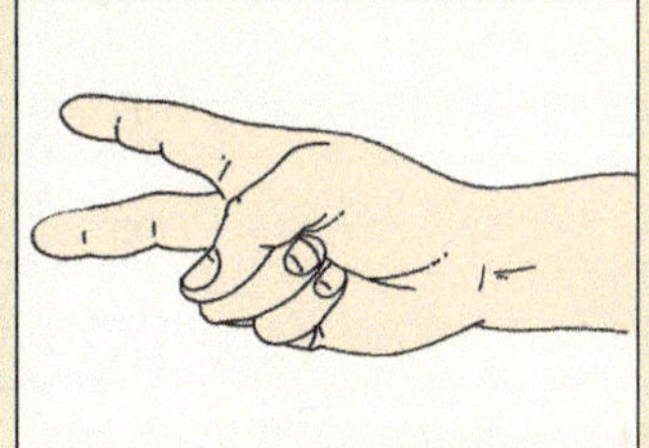
Scissors

4. When the two players make two different gestures, who wins? Rock **beats** scissors. Scissors beats paper. Paper beats rock. Sometimes **both** players make the same gesture. Then nobody wins.

5. Each time the players make their gestures, it's a "throw." There have to be three or more throws in a game. The player who wins two out of three throws is the winner.

6. Many people play the game just for fun, but sometimes it's a way to **decide** something—which movie to watch, for example, or what kind of pizza to get. The winner will be the one who decides. The game is sometimes used to decide more important things, too.

7. Rock, Paper, Scissors is easy to learn, fun to play, and free. **Try** it with a friend. To learn more about the game, try looking online.

Quick Comprehension Check

A. Read these sentences **about the reading**. Circle T (true) or F (false). On the line, write the number of the paragraph with the answer.

1. Rock, Paper, Scissors is a game just for children. T F _____
2. People play this game in many places. T F _____
3. A person needs to use two hands to play. T F _____
4. One player goes first and then the other player. T F _____
5. You can learn more about this game on the Internet. T F _____

B. Work with your class. Share your answers from part A. Go back to the reading to show why a sentence is true or false. Correct the false sentences.

EXPLORING VOCABULARY

Thinking about the Target Vocabulary

A. Find the words in **bold** in "An Easy Game" on page 63. Write them in the list. Use alphabetical order.

1. _around_
2. _____________
3. _____________
4. _____________
5. _____________
6. _____________
7. _____________
8. _____________
9. _____________
10. _____________

B. Circle the words in the list that are new to you. Then go back to the reading. Look for the words you circled. What do you think they mean?

Understanding the Target Vocabulary

A. Complete the sentences with the words in the box. The sentences are **about the reading**.

around	beats	both	decide	rules	try

1. People play Rock, Paper, Scissors in many different countries. You can find the game all ________________ the world.

2. Every game has ________________. They say what the players can and cannot do.

Vocabulary Tip: In the phrase *around the world*, *around* means "in many parts of." *Around* has other meanings, too. Find them in your dictionary.

3. The rules of the game say, "Rock _________________ scissors." This

   means that when I throw rock and you throw scissors, I win.

4. Sometimes the two players make the same gesture. For example,

   _________________ players throw paper.

5. Two friends want to watch a movie. He wants to watch one movie,

   and she wants to watch a different movie. They can play Rock,

   Paper, Scissors to _________________ which movie to watch.

6. When you _________________ a new game, you play it for the first time.

   Maybe you'll like it and maybe you won't.

Vocabulary Tip: Use *both* when you mean the two people (or things) in a group of two. Use *all* when you mean every person (or thing) in a group of three or more.

B. Complete the sentences about the picture. Write *each, holding, standing,* or *world.*

These three athletes come from different parts of the

_________________. _________________ athlete is
      (1)   (2)

_________________ and _________________ a ball.
   (3)   (4)

C. Complete the sentences with the words in the box.

both	decide	each	rules	stand	world

1. We have 20 students and 20 pencils. There is one pencil for

   _________________ student.

2. This is a big bowl. You need to hold it in _________________ hands.

3. It is not easy to learn the spelling _________________ for English words.

4. I like both kinds of pizza, so you can _________________ which kind we get.

5. Is Tokyo the biggest city in the _________________?

6. Sometimes there are a lot of people on the bus and there's no place to sit, so

   I have to _________________.

D. Complete the conversations with the words in the box.

around	beating	hold	try

1. A: Are the Red Sox winning the game?

   B: Yes, Boston is _________________ the Yankees, 5 to 4.

2. A: Can I help you with those bags?

   B: Would you just _________________ the door open for me? Thanks!

3. A: Can you help me with my French homework?

   B: I'll _________________ to help you, but I don't

   know much French.

4. A: What does the word "island" mean?

   B: An island is a place with water all

   _________________ it.

An island

DEVELOPING YOUR READING SKILLS

The Topic and the Main Idea

A. Go back to page 63 and read "An Easy Game" again.

B. Answer the questions about the topic and the main idea of the reading.
1. What is "An Easy Game" about? Check (✔) the topic.
   ☐ a. Games on the Internet
   ☐ b. Rock, Paper, Scissors
   ☐ c. Games around the world
2. What does the reading say about the topic? Check (✔) the main idea.
   ☐ a. Rock, Paper, Scissors is a game with just a few easy rules.
   ☐ b. Young and old people can play the same games.
   ☐ c. People know Rock, Paper, Scissors in many places.

Scanning

Scan the reading on page 63. Find the words to complete the sentences.

1. Rock, Paper, Scissors is called Ching Chong Cha in _________________.

2. The same game is called Ca-Chi-Pun in _________________.

3. The same game is called Kawi Bawi Bo in _________________.

4. Both _________________ people and _________________ people play this game.

5. The _________________ of the game are easy to learn.

6. Each player uses his or her hand to make a _________________.

7. People play the game for fun or as a way to _________________ something.

8. You can find out more about the game on the _________________.

Using a Diagram

Complete the diagram. Write the names of the three gestures in the correct order.

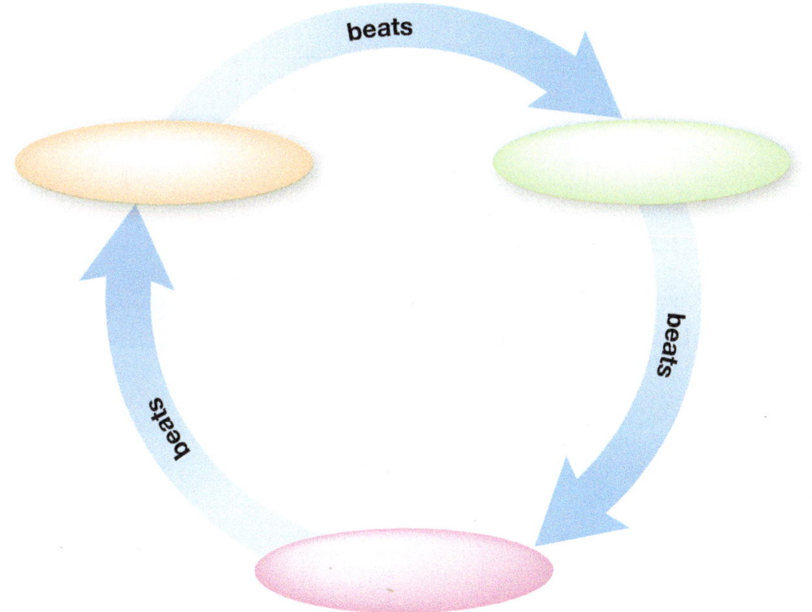

CRITICAL THINKING

Discussion

Talk about these questions with your class.

1. The reading says that many people play Rock, Paper, Scissors. Who are these people? Underline all the information in the reading that helps you answer this question. Do people in your country know this game? Do you know other names for it?

2. What are the rules of the game? Tell how many players there are, what they have to do, and how someone wins the game.

3. The reading says, "They have to make the gestures at the same time" (paragraph 2). Who are "they"? Why is it important for the gestures to happen at the same time?

4. Underline the part of the reading about why people play Rock, Paper, Scissors. Look again at the photo on page 62. Who is playing the game? Why do you think they are playing?

5. Sometimes you can find the writer's opinion in a reading. What does the writer of "An Easy Game" think about Rock, Paper, Scissors? What does the writer want readers to do? What is your opinion of the game?

WRITING

A. Use the Target Vocabulary: Complete the sentences. Copy your sentences on a piece of paper. Then find a partner, and read your partner's sentences.

1. I know the **rules** for _________________________________.

2. **Both** my mother and my father _________________________________.

3. I want to **try** to _________________________________.

4. I think I can **beat** _________________________________.

5. _________________________________ **around** the **world**.

B. Practice Listening and Writing: Get ready for a dictation. Practice writing these sentences. Then close your book. Take a piece of paper. Your teacher will say the sentences. Listen and write the sentences.

1. Each player knows the rules.
2. Both players move at the same time.
3. Hold your hand like this.
4. Try to win the game.
5. I think I can beat you.

C. Writing Practice: Circle the verb that is true for you. Then copy your sentences on a piece of paper. Find a partner, and read your partner's sentences.

1. I (like / don't like) to play games.

2. Rock, Paper, Scissors (is / isn't) an easy game to win.

3. The rules of the game (are / aren't) easy to learn.

4. People in my country (know / don't know) this game.

5. I ('d like / wouldn't like) to play Rock, Paper, Scissors.

CHAPTER 8

A New and Different Sport

Get that disc!

LEARNING OUTCOME
› Learn about a fast-growing sport

GETTING READY TO READ

Talk about these questions with your class.

1. Look at the photo. What do you see?

2. Match the names and pictures of these sports: *baseball, basketball, football, skating, soccer, tennis.*

a. ___________   b. ___________   c. ___________   d. ___________   e. ___________   f. ___________

3. Do you like any of these sports?

Read to Find Out: How is ultimate different from other sports?

Look at the words and pictures next to the reading. Then read. Do not stop to use a dictionary.

A New and Different Sport

1   Does everyone in the world know soccer? It **seems** that way! Most people know basketball, too. Not as many people know ultimate because it's a new sport. It's like other **team** sports in many ways, but in one important way, it's very different.

2   Ultimate, like soccer, is played on a big **field**. There are two teams, and each team has seven players. One team tries to get the disc[1] to the other end of the field. The other team tries to stop them. The player holding the disc cannot run with it. He or she has to stop and throw it. That player's teammates[2] run and try to **catch** the disc. Ultimate players, like soccer and basketball players, do a lot of running.

3   All sports have rules, but sometimes a player does not play by the rules. What **happens** then? In soccer or basketball, a referee[3] stops the game. It's the referee's job to tell the players what to do next. Ultimate is different. There are no referees. The players stop the game and talk about the **problem**. They have to **agree** on what to do next. Then the game can **continue**.

4   Today, men and women in more than 40 countries **enjoy** playing ultimate. It's a great game for children, too. It helps them learn how to solve[4] problems and play fair.[5] The sport is growing fast. Maybe there is a game of ultimate happening **somewhere** near you.

[1] an ultimate disc

[2] a teammate = a player on the same team

[3] a referee

[4] solve = find an answer to

[5] play fair = play without breaking the rules

Quick Comprehension Check

A. Read these sentences **about the reading**. Circle T (true) or F (false). On the line, write the number of the paragraph with the answer.

1.   Many people do not know about the game of ultimate. T   F   _____

2.   Ultimate is a game for two players with a disc.   T   F   _____

3.   The player holding the disc runs with it.   T   F   _____

4.   People play ultimate only in the United States.   T   F   _____

5.   People play ultimate with no referees.   T   F   _____

B. Work with your class. Share your answers from part A. Go back to the reading to show why a sentence is true or false. Correct the false sentences.

EXPLORING VOCABULARY

Thinking about the Target Vocabulary

A. Find the words in **bold** in "A New and Different Sport" on page 70. Write them in the list. Use alphabetical order.

1. _____agree_____   6. _______________

2. _______________   7. _______________

3. _______________   8. _______________

4. _______________   9. _______________

5. _______________   10. _______________

B. Circle the words in the list that are new to you. Then go back to the reading. Look for the words you circled. What do you think they mean?

Understanding the Target Vocabulary

A. Complete the sentences with the words in the box. The sentences are **about the reading**.

agree	continue	enjoy	problem	seems	somewhere

1. It isn't really true that everyone in the world knows soccer. It just

   _______________ true.

2. Sometimes a player doesn't play by the rules. That is a _______________.

   It's not right, and it makes the other team unhappy.

3. When there is a problem, ultimate players stop the game and talk.

   They have to _______________ on what to do about the problem.

   They need to have the same idea about what to do.

> **Vocabulary Tip:** When people do not agree, we say they disagree. *Agree* and *disagree* are opposites, like *up* and *down* or *fast* and *slow*.

4. After the two players agree, the game can _______________ .

   The two teams start playing again.

5. People in more than 40 countries like playing ultimate. Many men like

   this sport, and many women _______________ it, too.

6. People play ultimate in many places. Maybe there is a game

   _______________ near you right now.

B. Complete the sentences about the picture. Write *catch, field, happening,* or *teams.*

What is _________________ in the picture? It shows
(1)

two boys from two different baseball _________________.
(2)

They are on the _________________. One boy is trying to
(3)

_________________ the ball.
(4)

C. Complete the sentences with the words in the box.

catch	continue	enjoy	field	team

1. People play both soccer and ultimate on a long _________________.

2. A soccer _________________ has 11 players on the field.

3. I like to go see new places, but I don't _________________ flying.

4. Use both hands to _________________ the ball.

5. We'll stop for a few minutes when we get tired. Then we'll

   _________________ working.

D. Complete the conversations with the words in the box.

agree	happening	problem	seem	somewhere

1. A: I think we need a computer. What do you think?

   B: I _________________. We need one.

2. A: Ed and Marta _________________ happy.

   B: Yes, they do, but they really aren't.

3. A: Why is Robert taking the bus, not his car?

   B: He's having a _________________ with his car.

4. A: Can I call you back later? I'm watching the game.

   B: What's _________________? Who's winning?

5. A: What are you looking for?

   B: My pen. It's in my bag _________________, but I can't find it.

DEVELOPING YOUR READING SKILLS

The Topic and the Main Idea

A. Go back to page 70 and read "A New and Different Sport" again.

B. Answer the questions about the topic and the main idea of the reading.

1. What is "A New and Different Sport" about? Check (✔) the topic.
   - ☐ a. The sport of ultimate
   - ☐ b. Sports around the world
   - ☐ c. Team sports

2. What does the reading say about the topic? Check (✔) the main idea.
   - ☐ a. More people know the sport of soccer than ultimate.
   - ☐ b. In the game of ultimate, there is a lot of running and throwing the disc.
   - ☐ c. Ultimate is like soccer and basketball in some ways, but it's very different, too.

Giving Details

Answer these questions about the reading.

1. What two other examples of team sports does the reading give?

   _________________ and _________________

2. How many people play on an ultimate team? _________________

3. What does the player with the disc try to do? _________________

4. In soccer or basketball, whose job is it to start and stop the game?

   ____

5. Who starts and stops the game in ultimate? _________________

6. Is ultimate a game for men, for women, or for both men and women?

   ____

7. How many countries have people that play ultimate? _________________

Summarizing the Reading

Complete the summary of the reading on page 70. Use *catch, disc, field, referees,* or *team.*

Ultimate is a fast-growing sport. It is a ________________ sport, like
(1)

soccer and basketball. Ultimate is played on a ________________, like soccer.
(2)

One team tries to get the ________________ to the other end of the field. The
(3)

other team tries to stop them. Players have to throw and ________________
(4)

the disc. There is a lot of running in ultimate, as in basketball and soccer.

Ultimate is different from those two sports in one important way. There are

no ________________.
(5)

CRITICAL THINKING

Discussion

Talk about these questions in a small group.

1. How are ultimate and soccer the same? Write your answers in the part of the diagram under Both. How are the two sports different? Write your answers under each sport.

Critical Thinking Tip:
The diagram on this page is called a Venn diagram. Use a diagram like this to compare two things—to show how they are the same and how they are different.

ULTIMATE   BOTH   SOCCER

2. Name some other sports for two teams: ________________________________

____

Name some sports for two players: ________________________________

____

Now think about people playing these sports with no referees. What kinds of problems might there be? What would the players have to do? What would it be like for the people who are watching the sport? Do you think it would be a good idea to play the game without referees? Tell why or why not.

3. What is the writer's opinion about children playing ultimate? What does the writer think children can learn from playing ultimate? How can playing ultimate help them learn these things? Do you agree with the writer?

WRITING

A. Use the Target Vocabulary: Complete the sentences. Copy your sentences on a piece of paper. Then find a partner, and read your partner's sentences.

1. I **enjoy** watching _________________.

2. People play _________________ on a **field**.

3. Sometimes I have **problems** with _________________.

4. _________________ and I sometimes don't **agree** about _________________.

5. What **happens** when _________________?

B. Practice Listening and Writing: Get ready for a dictation. Practice writing these sentences. Then close your book. Take a piece of paper. Your teacher will say the sentences. Listen and write the sentences.

1. People play sports around the world.

2. Many people enjoy watching sports.

3. Do you watch sports on TV?

4. Do you have a favorite sport?

C. Writing Practice: Write your answers to these questions on a piece of paper. Then find a partner, and read your partner's sentences.

1. What sports do people like in your country?

2. Do you like to play sports?

3. Do you watch sports on TV?

4. Do you have a favorite sport?

Examples:

1. People in my country like soccer and auto racing.
2. I don't like to play sports.
3. I sometimes watch the Olympics on TV.
4. I don't have a favorite sport.

CHAPTER 9

Collectors

Two collectors of trading cards

LEARNING OUTCOME

> Learn about collecting things

GETTING READY TO READ

Talk about these questions with your class.

1. Look at the photo. What do you see?
2. Do you know people who collect any of these things?

butterflies

teddy bears

earrings

3. What other kinds of things do people collect?

Read to Find Out: What kinds of people like to collect things?

Look at the words and pictures next to the reading. Then read. Do not stop to use a dictionary.

Collectors

1   Many people like to **collect** things. They collect all kinds of things, from coins[1] to teacups to cookbooks to cars. Why do they do it? Most collectors will tell you, "Because it's fun." A few will say, "I **hope** to make some money."

[1] *coins*

2   Other people may **laugh** and say, "Collecting? No, that's not for me! I don't **care** about that kind of thing." Is what they say really true? Many of us collect things **without** thinking about it.

3   Small children don't think about it, but they are natural[2] collectors. They **pick up** little things they see. For example, a little boy finds a nice stone or a shell.[3] Then he finds some more. He **carries** them home, and that's the start of a collection.

[2] *natural* = needing no teaching

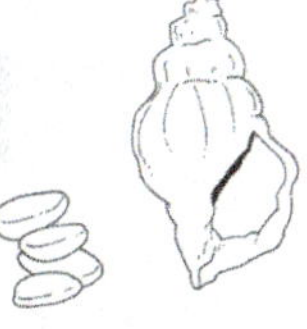

4   Older children collect things, too—teddy bears, for example. Some collect trading cards with pictures of their favorite athletes.[4] Many enjoy collecting the same things as their friends. When they get something new, they want to tell their friends about it and show them. These children enjoy playing with their things **together**.

[3] *stones* and a *shell*

[4] *athletes* = people who play sports

5   Men and women may collect things that make them **remember** being children, like comic books. A new comic book doesn't cost much, but some people will pay a lot for an old one. In 1938, the first Superman comic book cost **only** $.10 (ten cents), but in 2014, a collector bought[5] one of those first Superman comics online for more than $2,000,000.

[5] *bought* = the simple past of *buy*

Reading a comic book

6   Are you a collector? Maybe your answer at first is no, but think again. Maybe you have a lot of photos, music, earrings, or T-shirts that say something. Then you are a collector, too.

Quick Comprehension Check

A. Read these sentences **about the reading**. Circle T (true) or F (false). On the line, write the number of the paragraph with the answer.

1. A collector has many things of the same kind.   T   F   _____

2. Men, women, and children can be collectors.   T   F   _____

3. You need a lot of money to be a collector.   T   F   _____

4. Many children enjoy showing their collections to their friends.   T   F   _____

5. Most collectors try to get a lot of money for their things.   T   F   _____

B. Work with your class. Share your answers from part A. Go back to the reading to show why a sentence is true or false. Correct the false sentences.

EXPLORING VOCABULARY

Thinking about the Target Vocabulary

A. Find the words in **bold** in "Collectors" on page 77. Write them in the list. Use alphabetical order.

1. _____*care*_____   6. _____________

2. _____________   7. _____________

3. _____________   8. _____________

4. _____________   9. _____________

5. _____________   10. _____________

B. Circle the words in the list that are new to you. Then go back to the reading. Look for the words you circled. What do you think they mean?

Understanding the Target Vocabulary

A. Complete the sentences with the words in the box. The sentences are **about the reading**.

care	collect	hope	only	remember	together	without

1. Many people like to _________________ things. This means to get a lot of things of one kind and put them all in one place.

2. Some people collect things because they _________________ to make money. They want this to happen.

> **Vocabulary Tip:** A person who collects things is called a collector. The group of things that the person collects is called a collection.

3. Some people say, "Collecting things isn't important to me. I don't

   _________________ about that."

4. Many of us collect things, but we do not think about what we're doing.

   We do it _________________ thinking about making a collection.

5. Most children like to play with others. They like to play

   _________________.

6. Some people collect things that make them _________________ being

   children. These people think back to the time when they were young.

7. In 1938, the first Superman comic book did not cost much.

   It cost _________________ ten cents.

> **Vocabulary Tip:** *Only* and *just* are **synonyms** (words with the same meaning).

B. Complete the sentences about the pictures. Write *carrying, laughing,* or *picking up.*

1. She is _________________ a shell from the beach.

> **Vocabulary Tip:** *Carry* means "hold something as you take it somewhere."

2. He is _________________ some boxes.

3. They are _________________.

C. Complete the conversations with the words in the box.

carry	laughing	only	remember	without

1. A: Do you know that girl?

   B: Yes, but I can't _________________ her name.

2. A: Would you like some help?

   B: Thanks! I need to _________________ these boxes up to the fourth

   floor.

3. A: Ha ha ha ha ha!

   B: What's so funny? Why are you _________________?

4. A: Is it cold today?

   B: Yes, it is. Don't go out _________________ a coat and hat.

5. A: Is the game on TV now?

   B: No, the game's at 4:00. It's _________________ 3:30.

D. Complete the sentences with the words in the box.

care	collects	hope	pick up	together

1. The players on a team need to work _________________.

2. Soccer players use their feet. They cannot _________________ the ball
   with their hands.

3. My father _________________ stamps from around the world.

4. I _________________ my team will win.

5. The only thing she seems to _________________ about is money.

> **Writing Tip:** Use *about* after *care*: *I care about my family and friends.*

DEVELOPING YOUR READING SKILLS

The Topic and the Main Idea

A. Go back to page 77 and read "Collectors" again.

B. Answer the questions about the topic and the main idea of the reading.

1. What is "Collectors" about? Check (✔) the topic.
    - ☐ a. Collecting for children
    - ☐ b. People who collect things
    - ☐ c. Making money from a collection
2. What does the reading say about the topic? Check (✔) the main idea.
    - ☐ a. Collecting is fun for many men, women, and children.
    - ☐ b. Collectors are people with a lot of money and free time.
    - ☐ c. There are a few easy rules for starting a collection.

Finding Examples

Complete the chart. Give examples from the reading, and think of more examples of your own.

		Collectors		
		Small children	Older children	Men and women
Examples of things that people collect	From the reading	*little stones* *shells*		
	Your ideas			

Giving Details

Answer these questions about the reading.

1. Why do most people collect things? _______________________________________

2. What do some people hope to get from collecting things? ____________________

3. Why do some people collect comic books?___________________________________

4. How much did someone pay for a 1938 Superman comic book? ________________

5. Where did the person buy the comic book? _________________________________

6. In what year did this happen? ____

CRITICAL THINKING

Discussion

Talk about these questions with your class.

1. Who does the writer call "natural collectors?" What does this phrase mean? Why do men and women collect things? Underline all the answers you can find in the reading. Can you think of any other reasons?

2. Read paragraph 4 again. What is the main idea of this paragraph? What details does the writer give to support the main idea? Do you agree that children usually like to enjoy their collections with their friends? Do you think this is true for men and women who collect things? Tell why or why not. Give examples.

> **Critical Thinking Tip:**
> Giving examples is one way you can support an opinion (show why you think it's true).

3. What does the writer say about "many of us" in paragraph 2? Where in the reading does the writer return to this idea? Do you agree with the writer's opinion? Tell why or why not.

4. Are you a collector? What do you collect now? What do you think would be fun to collect?

WRITING

A. Use the Target Vocabulary: Complete the sentences. Copy your sentences on a piece of paper. Then find a partner, and read your partner's sentences.

1. I **carry** ______________________ in my (backpack / wallet / handbag).

2. I would like to **collect** ______________________.

3. It is sometimes hard for me to **remember** ______________________.

4. I **hope** to ______________________ tomorrow.

5. I **laugh** when ______________________.

B. Practice Listening and Writing: Get ready for a dictation. Practice writing these sentences. Then close your book. Take a piece of paper. Your teacher will say the sentences. Listen and write the sentences.

1. People collect all kinds of things.
2. Small children pick up little things.
3. Many men and women are collectors.
4. Some of them spend a lot of money.

C. Writing Practice: Give one or more answers to each question. Write your sentences on a piece of paper. Then find a partner and read your partner's sentences.

1. What, or who, makes you laugh?
2. What do you and your friends like to do together?
3. What will you always remember?

Examples:

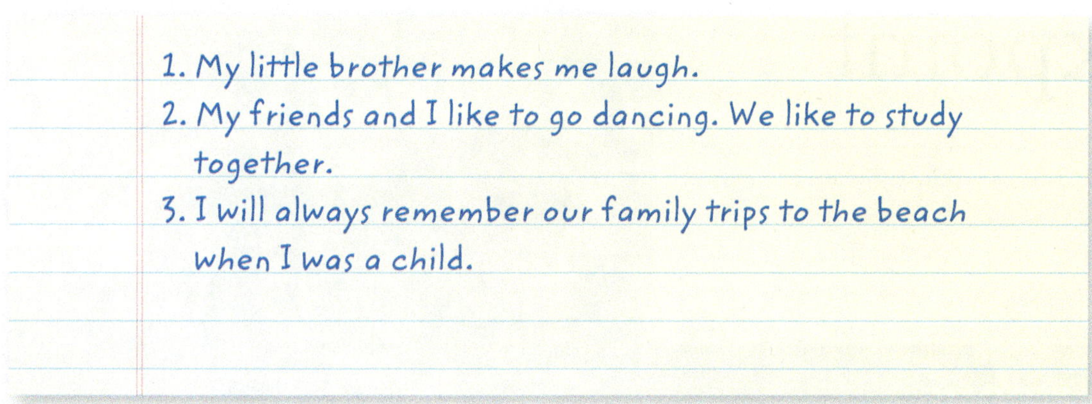

Checkpoint

LEARNING OUTCOME

> Review and expand on the content of Unit 3

LOOK BACK

A. Think About This

Look back at your answers to the *Think About This* question on page 61:

What do you like to do for fun?

Would you like to add anything?

B. Remember the Readings

What do you want to remember from the readings in Unit 3? For each chapter, write one sentence about the reading.

Chapter 7: An Easy Game

____

Chapter 8: A New and Different Sport

____

Chapter 9: Collectors

____

REVIEWING VOCABULARY

Write the correct word to complete the sentence.

1. There are 12 students and 12 computers. That means one computer for
   _________________ student.
   - **a.** both
   - **b.** each
   - **c.** catch

2. The players on a team all have to work _________________.
   - **a.** rule
   - **b.** field
   - **c.** together

3. Anna _________________ happy today.
   - **a.** seems
   - **b.** beats
   - **c.** problems

4. You need to learn the _________________ to play the game.
   - **a.** rules
   - **b.** worlds
   - **c.** laughs

5. I like it when good things _________________ to nice people.
   - **a.** remember
   - **b.** carry
   - **c.** happen

6. I _________________ that we'll have nice weather this weekend.
   - **a.** enjoy
   - **b.** hope
   - **c.** collect

7. They _________________ their little boy and carry him when he is tired of
   walking.
   - **a.** try
   - **b.** pick up
   - **c.** team

8. Will you please _________________ the baby for me?
   - **a.** decide
   - **b.** agree
   - **c.** hold

9. Classes end in May. They don't _________________ after May 15.
   - **a.** care
   - **b.** continue
   - **c.** stand

10. Tina always makes me laugh. I can't listen to her _________________
    laughing!
    - **a.** only
    - **b.** somewhere
    - **c.** without

EXPANDING VOCABULARY

Nouns

There are many different kinds of words. A **noun** is one kind of word. Most nouns can be singular (*book*) or plural (*books*).

What Is a Noun?		Examples of Nouns
Nouns are words for	people:	*boy, police, drivers, George*
	places:	*airport, classroom, fields, Tokyo*
	things:	*bicycle, pen, bowls, Honda*
	ideas:	*time, love, feelings, size*

Each sentence has one noun. Find and circle the noun.

1. She is a good student.
2. Do you eat a big breakfast?
3. They are beginners.
4. You are a fast learner.
5. My team is winning.
6. What is in the box?
7. I think it is a good plan.
8. Why is Peter laughing?
9. Would you like a snack?
10. They are flying around the world.

A PUZZLE

Complete these sentences with words you studied in Chapters 7–9. Look at the word lists on pages 64, 71, and 78 for help. Write the words in the puzzle.

ACROSS

1. I like my coffee black. That means w_______________ milk or cream.

2. I like that actor, but I can't r_______________ his name.

3. Before they practice, the players run a_______________ the field.

5. I will t_______________ to get there early.

6. I e_______________ watching sports on TV.

7. I h_______________ you have a good time at the party.

8. His stories always make me l_______________.

DOWN

1. They are flying around the _______world_______.

3. She thinks they can spend the money, but her husband does not

   a_______________.

4. Henry has two sisters, and they are b_______________ in college.

5. Fatima and Carmen ride the bus t_______________.

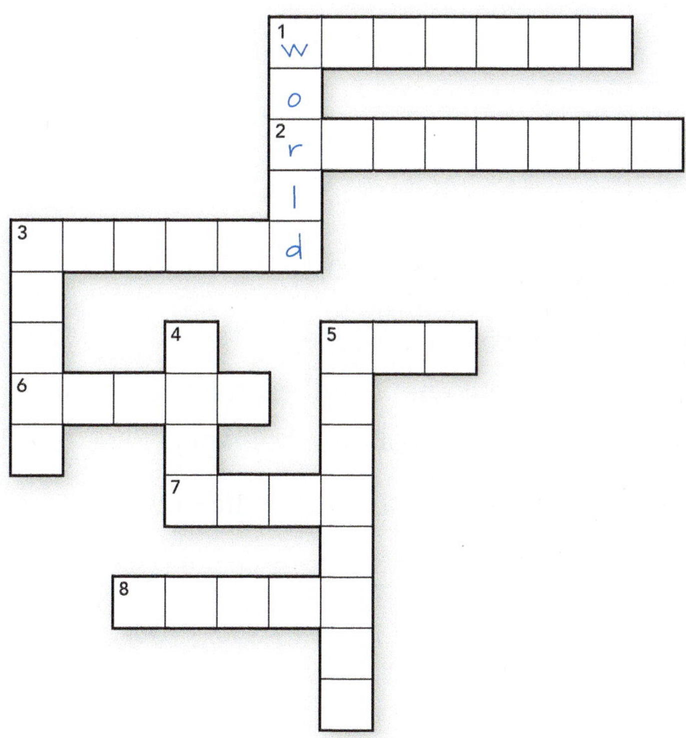

Do You Like Puzzles?

1   Puzzles can be a lot of fun. There are many different kinds. Some use pictures. Some use words or numbers. Three popular[1] kinds are jigsaw, crossword, and Sudoku puzzles.

[1] *popular* = liked by many people

2   A jigsaw puzzle has many small pieces. A piece looks something like this:

Each piece has a part of a picture on it. Put all the pieces together and you will see the picture.

3   On page 87, there is a crossword puzzle. It's a game of words. This kind of puzzle is very popular in the United States. You can find crosswords in newspapers and on the Internet. Millions[2] of people try to do the crosswords in *The New York Times* newspaper.

[2] *a million* = 1,000,000

4   You can find Sudoku puzzles in newspapers and online, too. Sudoku puzzles use numbers. Here is an example of a Sudoku puzzle.

Here are the rules for Sudoku puzzles:

- Write the numbers 1 to 9 in the boxes.
- Use all 9 numbers in each row, each column, and each block.
- Use each number just one time in a row, column, or block.

5   The rules are easy, but the puzzles may not be. Try to do the one on this page.

Comprehension Check

Read these sentences about the reading. Circle T (true) or F (false). On the line, write the number of the paragraph with the answer. Correct the false sentences.

1. There are many different kinds of puzzles.   T   F   ____
2. There are crossword puzzles in this book.   T   F   ____
3. You can find jigsaw puzzles in U.S. newspapers.   T   F   ____
4. A Sudoku puzzle is a game of words.   T   F   ____
5. You need to learn many rules to do a   T   F   ____
   Sudoku puzzle.

Scanning

Find the words to complete the sentences about the reading.

1. A puzzle may use pictures, _________________, or _________________.

2. A jigsaw puzzle has many small _________________.

3. A _________________ puzzle is a game of words.

4. You can find crossword puzzles in _________________ and on the

   _________________.

5. Sudoku puzzles use _________________.

6. Write the numbers from _________________ to _________________ in the
   boxes of a Sudoku puzzle.

Topics of Paragraphs

Match the paragraphs and their topics. Write each paragraph topic in the right place.

Do You Like Puzzles?	
Paragraph 1	kinds of puzzles
Paragraph 2	
Paragraph 3	
Paragraph 4	
Paragraph 5	

Topics of Paragraphs
__ a Sudoku puzzle for you
__ Sudoku puzzles
__ jigsaw puzzles
__ crossword puzzles
✔ kinds of puzzles

The Main Idea of the Reading

What is the main idea of "Do You Like Puzzles?" Check (✔) your answer.

- ☐ a. You can find crosswords and Sudoku puzzles in newspapers and online.
- ☐ b. Three popular kinds of puzzles are jigsaw, crossword, and Sudoku puzzles.
- ☐ c. Puzzles are fun for people young and old.

Critical Thinking

Talk about these questions with your class.

1. The reading describes three different kinds of puzzles. Which one is a game of words? Which one is a game of numbers? Which one breaks a picture into many small pieces? Do you enjoy any of these three kinds of puzzles? Which kind do you think is the easiest, and which kind do you think is the hardest?

2. Why did the writer write "Do You Like Puzzles?" Check (✔) your answer.

    - ☐ a. The writer wants to make readers laugh.
    - ☐ b. The write wants readers to go buy some puzzles.
    - ☐ c. The writer wants to give readers information they may not know.

    Tell which answer you checked and why.

3. Many people begin puzzles but then don't finish them. Why do you think that happens?

FRIENDS

THINK ABOUT THIS

Complete this sentence. Check (✓) three answers only.

A friend is someone who . . .

- [ ] is fun to do things with.
- [ ] likes the same things you do.
- [ ] knows you very well.
- [ ] is a good listener.
- [ ] tells you everything.
- [ ] Your idea: ___________________________

Good Friends and Good Health

Friends

LEARNING OUTCOME

> Learn about how friends are good for you

GETTING READY TO READ

Talk about these questions with your class.

1. The chapter title is "Good Friends and Good Health." Look at the two friends in the photo. In what ways do you think they may be good for each other's health?

2. In what ways do you think your friendships[1] are good for you?

[1] *friendships* = relationships between friends

Read to Find Out: How are your friends good for you?

Look at the words and picture next to the reading. Then read. Do not stop to use a dictionary.

Good Friends and Good Health

1   Look for the word *friend* in an English dictionary. You will see something like this:

> **friend** /frɛnd/ *noun* a person who you know and like and enjoy spending time with

This definition of the word doesn't tell you one important thing about friends. They're good for your **health**. Here are three ways that is true.

2   • *People with good friends don't **get** sick as much.*

Your doctor may tell you that **if** a person has good friends, they don't get colds[1] as **often**. Research[2] shows this to be true. Having friends helps in some bigger ways, too. For example, people with **strong** friendships don't have as many **heart** problems. They also don't have as many problems with high blood pressure.[3]

3   • *People with good friends live longer.*

Research in Australia shows that people with strong friendships live longer than people without them. The doctors who did the research learned that for long life, friends are more important than families. Does that **surprise** you?

4   • *People with good friends are happier.*

When **life** is good, it's great to get together and laugh with our friends. But we also need friends when times are bad. Sometimes our friends can do something to help us. At other times, they can only listen. That helps, too. When you're **sad**, it feels good to talk with a friend who **understands**, doesn't it? Talking with friends helps people live happier lives.

5   Our lives can get very busy, with school and work and the needs of our families. It can be hard to find time for friends. But we need to remember that friendship is important, too. Our friends are good for us, and we're good for them.

[1] *He has a cold.*

[2] *research =* study of a subject done to learn new facts or test ideas

[3] *high blood pressure =* when your heart is having to work very hard

Quick Comprehension Check

A. Read these sentences **about the reading**. Circle T (true) or F (false). On the line, write the number of the paragraph with the answer.

1. Doctors say having friends is good for you.   T   F   ____

2. People with good friends have more heart problems.   T   F   ____

3. Having good friends will help you live a long life.   T   F   ____

4. For a happy life, don't talk about your problems.   T   F   ____

5. Having good friends makes you happier.   T   F   ____

B. Work with your class. Share your answers from part A. Go back to the reading to show why a sentence is true or false. Correct the false sentences.

EXPLORING VOCABULARY

Thinking about the Target Vocabulary

A. Find the words in **bold** in "Good Friends and Good Health" on page 93. Write them in the list. Use alphabetical order.

1. _____get_____   6. __________

2. __________   7. __________

3. __________   8. __________

4. __________   9. __________

5. __________   10. __________

B. Circle the words in the list that are new to you. Find those words in the reading. Can you guess their meanings?

Understanding the Target Vocabulary

A. Complete the sentences with the words in the box. The sentences are **about the reading**.

getting	health	if	life	often	understand

1. Friends are good for your __________. Having good friends helps you feel good and not be sick.

2. When you are __________ sick, that means you are starting to be sick.

> **Vocabulary Tip:** *Get* has many meanings. *Get* + a noun can mean "buy" (*I'll get bread at the store*) or "find" (*Get help!*). *Get* + an adjective means "start to be" (*Are you getting tired?*).

3. Some people have a lot of friends. Is that true for you? _________________

   that is true for you, then maybe you don't get a lot of colds.

4. Some people never seem to get sick. Other people _________________ get

   sick. It happens to them a lot.

5. When things are going well for you and you're happy, you can

   say "_________________ is good."

6. When you talk to a friend about your problems, you hope that your friend

   will _________________. You want your friend to know how you are feeling.

B. Complete the sentences about the pictures. Write *heart, sad, strong,* or *surprised.*

1. She feels _________________ to say good-bye.

2. Love is a very _________________ feeling.

3. The doctor is listening to the man's _____________.

4. He didn't know what was in the box. It

   _________________ him.

C. Complete the conversations with the words in the box.

getting	if	strong	surprises	understand

1. **A:** Do you feel okay? You look tired.

   B: I think I'm _________________ sick.

2. **A:** Are you going to go to the park this weekend?

   B: _________________ the weather is nice, then yes, I will, but it might rain.

3. **A:** I don't like ice cream.

   B: Really? That _________________ me. Doesn't everybody like ice cream?

4. **A:** I don't know this word. I don't _________________ what it means. Do you?

   B: I'm afraid not. I'll find it in the dictionary.

5. **A:** Does Don always tell everybody what he thinks about everything?

   B: Yes, he does! He's a man of _________________ opinions.

D. Complete the sentences with the words in the box.

health	heart	lives	often	sad

1. Is there some problem? You look _________________.

2. Marco is 60, but he's in very good _________________ and seems younger.

3. I _________________ see Nina because we're in the same class.

4. If your _________________ usually beats 60 times a minute, does that mean it's good and strong?

5. Many people enjoy reading about the _________________ of rich and famous people.

DEVELOPING YOUR READING SKILLS

The Topic and the Main Idea

A. Go back to page 93 and read "Good Friends and Good Health" again.

B. Answer the questions about the topic and the main idea of the reading.

1. What is "Good Friends and Good Health" about? Check (✔) the topic.
   - ☐ a. Ways to get healthy
   - ☐ b. The meaning of *friend*
   - ☐ c. How friends are good for you

2. What does the reading say about the topic? Check (✔) the main idea.
   - ☐ a. A friend is a person you enjoy spending time with.
   - ☐ b. Having good friends helps you be healthy and happy.
   - ☐ c. Friends are more important than families.

> **Reading Tip:** The reading in this chapter has a **bulleted list** (or bullet list). The three sentences in italics are the **bullet points**. Writers use bulleted lists to make information clear and easy to read.

Topics of Paragraphs

Match the paragraphs and their topics. Write each paragraph topic in the right place.

Our Friends and Our Health	
Paragraph 1	the meaning of friend
Paragraph 2	
Paragraph 3	
Paragraph 4	
Paragraph 5	

Topics of Paragraphs
__ friends and living a long life
✔ the meaning of *friend*
__ friends and health problems
__ finding time for friends
__ friends in good times and bad times

Reading for Details

Read the questions. Circle the answer that the reading gives. Circle "It doesn't say" if the reading does not give that information.

1.	Do doctors study the topic of friendship?	Yes	No	It doesn't say.
2.	Do strong friendships help us to be healthy?	Yes	No	It doesn't say.
3.	Are friends good for us in more than three ways?	Yes	No	It doesn't say.
4.	Are friends sometimes bad for us?	Yes	No	It doesn't say.

5. To live a long life, is family more important   Yes   No   It doesn't say.
   than friends?

6. Is it good for us to have friends who listen to us? Yes   No   It doesn't say.

7. Is talking on the phone the same as talking   Yes   No   It doesn't say.
   face-to-face?

CRITICAL THINKING

Discussion

Talk about these questions in a small group.

1. Look at the word *bigger* in paragraph 2. What does it mean in this sentence? The writer is using *bigger* to compare two different things. What is the writer comparing? Check your answer:

   ☐ a. Numbers of friends

   ☐ b. Kinds of heart problems

   ☐ c. Ways that having friends helps us

2. In paragraph 3, the reading compares families and friends. What does the reading say? Is this information the writer's opinion? What is your opinion about this information?

3. The reading says that having good friends is good for our physical health. (It's good for our bodies.) Underline an example. The reading also says that having good friends is good for our mental health. (It's good for the way we think and feel.) Underline an example. Is any of this information new to you? What do you want to know more about? Write a question you would like to ask about friendship and health.

4. The reading says nothing about friends being bad for you. Can you think of examples of how friends could be bad for someone's physical health (for the person's body) and examples of how they could be bad for someone's mental health (the way the person thinks)? Why are there no examples like these in the reading?

5. The writer says, "It can be hard to find time for friends" (paragraph 5). Do you agree? Underline the writer's examples of reasons why it can be hard. Are any of these reasons true for you? What other reasons can you think of?

> **Critical Thinking Tip:**
> When you compare two things, you show how they are the same or different. This sentence compares two brothers and shows how they are different: *Tom is older than Al.*

WRITING

A. Use the Target Vocabulary: Complete the sentences. Write your sentences on a piece of paper. Then find a partner, and read each other's sentences.

1. When I don't **understand** something in English, I _____________________.

2. I feel **sad** when I think about _____________________.

3. To live a happy **life**, you need _____________________.

4. **I often** _____________________.

5. **If** I win a million dollars, I will _____________________.

B. Writing Practice: Think of one or more answers to each question. On a piece of paper, write your sentences in the form of a paragraph. Then find a partner, and read your partner's paragraph.

1. How often do you see your friends?
2. How do you and your friends spend time together?
3. Do you think you have enough time with your friends?

> **Writing Tip:** When you write an opinion with *not*, use "I don't think" + your opinion: *I don't think I see my friends enough* (not: ~~I think I don't~~ *see my friends enough*).

Example:

Some of my friends live far away and I don't often see them. We talk on the phone or online sometimes. I see other friends at school every day. We like to eat together, and we do our homework together. We talk about a lot of different things. I don't think I have enough time with my friends. I would like to spend ALL my time with my friends.

CHAPTER 11

Being Honest with Friends

Do you want my honest opinion?

LEARNING OUTCOME

> Learn about honesty between friends

GETTING READY TO READ

Talk about these questions with your class.

1. When a person has a problem, sometimes they will write to someone whose job is giving advice.[1] Do you ever read letters in the newspaper or messages online that ask for advice? What kinds of problems do people ask for help with?

2. Being honest means saying only what is true. Is it important for friends to be honest? Read three sentences about friends and check (✔) the one you agree with. Explain your answer.

   ☐ You should always be honest with your friends.

   ☐ You should usually be honest with your friends.

   ☐ You don't have to be honest with your friends.

[1] *advice* = an opinion about what is the right thing for someone to do

Read to Find Out: What two opinions does the reading discuss?

Look at the words next to the reading. Then read. Do not stop to use a dictionary.

Being Honest with Friends

? Ask Anna!

Dear Anna,

My friend and I don't agree about something. I say friends always have to be honest and **tell the truth**. This is what it means to be a friend—you know your friend will always be open with you.

My friend says the truth can **hurt**, and you **should** never hurt a friend or anyone you care about.

Who do you think is right?

Jamie

1. *Ask Anna!* is the name of a newspaper advice column.[1] Jamie is asking Anna a good question. How would you answer it?

2. Most people agree that we want our friends to be honest. We **trust** them to tell us what they really think, and when we ask, "What do you think?," we want to know their opinions. We don't want to **worry** that our friends are lying[2] to us. Maybe Jamie is right: We want our friends to tell us the truth, **so** it's **better** for us to tell them the truth, too.

3. But do we really want to hear the truth, all the truth, all the time? As Jamie's friend says, the truth can hurt, and we also trust our friends not to hurt us. Maybe sometimes we ask a friend "What do you think?" but we aren't really ready to hear the truth. (At other times, maybe we don't ask that question because we're afraid to hear the answer.) So Jamie's friend may be right: A friend needs to be **careful** not to say something that will hurt.

4. We also need to think about what happens if you don't tell your friend the truth. That can be a problem because maybe later your friend will learn what you really think. Then your friend may feel both hurt and **angry**.

5. Jamie is asking a **difficult** question. What will Anna's answer be?

[1] *advice column* = part of a newspaper with advice for readers with problems

[2] *lying* = saying something that is not true

Quick Comprehension Check

A. Read these sentences **about the reading**. Circle T (true) or F (false). On the line, write the number of the paragraph with the answer.

1. Jamie wants some advice about what to do.   T   F   _____

2. Anna is a friend of Jamie's.   T   F   _____

3. Jamie says friends should always be honest.   T   F   _____

4. Jamie's friend agrees with Jamie.   T   F   _____

5. The reading gives Anna's opinion.   T   F   _____

B. Work with your class. Share your answers from part A. Go back to the reading to show why a sentence is true or false. Correct the false sentences.

EXPLORING VOCABULARY

Thinking about the Target Vocabulary

A. Find the words in **bold** in "Being Honest with Friends" on page 101. Write them in the list. Use alphabetical order.

1. _____*angry*_____   6. _______________

2. _______________   7. _______________

3. _______________   8. _______________

4. _______________   9. _______________

5. _______________   10. _______________

B. Circle the words in the list that are new to you. Find those words in the reading. Can you guess their meanings?

Understanding the Target Vocabulary

A. Complete the sentences with the words and phrases in the box. The sentences are **about the reading**.

better	careful	difficult	hurts	so	telling the truth	trust

1. When you say what is really true, you are _______________.

2. Jamie's friend says that you can make a friend feel bad if you tell the truth. Sometimes the truth _______________.

Vocabulary Tip: *Hurt* can be a verb (*If you fall, you'll hurt yourself*) or an adjective (*She feels hurt because you didn't call*).

3. When you are sure that your friends will not lie to you or do anything

   bad to you, then you can say that you _________________ your friends.

4. We want to know our friends' opinions, _________________ we ask them,

   "What do you think?" We ask because we want to know.

5. Is it always good to tell the truth, or is it sometimes _________________

   not to say what you think?

6. Sometimes it's easy to hurt a friend's feelings. If you don't want to

   hurt a friend, you need to think before you speak. You need to be

   _________________ what you say.

7. Jamie is asking a question that is not easy to answer. It's a

   _________________ question to answer.

B. Complete the sentences about the pictures. Write *angry, should,* or *worry.*

1. People _________________ when their children are sick.

2. Sam is _________________ because Mike's ice cream
   cone is bigger.

3. This sweater is too big. Tim _________________ get a
   smaller one.

C. Complete the questions with the words in the box.

are worrying about something	should I tell him	trust him
hurt someone	telling the truth	

1. How do you know if someone is

   ____?

2. Do you tell the truth if it will

   ____?

3. He says he will return the money, but do you

   ____?

4. He says he wants the truth from me, but

   ____?

5. Is it difficult for you to sleep when you

   ____?

D. Complete the sentences with the words in the box.

angry	better	careful	difficult	so

1. I need some information, __________________ I'm going to go online.

2. My father's heart isn't strong, so he needs to be __________________.

3. It's not easy to remember all the details. It's __________________.

4. It makes me __________________ when he laughs at my problems.

5. Don't go to school in the morning hungry. It's __________________

   to have a good breakfast.

Vocabulary Tip: *Better* is a form of *good.* Use *better* when you compare how good two things are: *His new movie is better than his last one.*

DEVELOPING YOUR READING SKILLS

The Topic and the Main Idea

A. Go back to page 101 and read "Being Honest with Friends" again.

B. Answer the questions about the topic and the main idea of the reading.

1. What is "Being Honest with Friends" about? Check (✔) the topic.

   ☐ a. Telling a friend the truth

   ☐ b. Asking friends for their opinions

   ☐ c. Getting advice

2. What does the reading say about the topic? Check (✔) the main idea.

   ☐ a. You should always tell your friends the truth.

   ☐ b. Sometimes it's a bad idea to tell your friends the truth.

   ☐ c. It's difficult to know if you should always tell friends the truth.

> **Reading Tip:** When you read something for the second time, that's the time to mark up the reading. Use a pencil to mark the parts you think are most important to remember.

Understanding Sentences with *Because*

> **Understanding Sentences with *Because***
>
> Sentences with *because* answer the question *Why?* The sentences have two parts. The part that starts with *because* is the reason.
>
> The reason can be the first or the second part of the sentence. When the reason is first, put a comma (,) after that part of the sentence.
>
> People write letters to Ask Anna **because they want advice.**
> **Because they want advice,** people write letters to Ask Anna.

Choose the best way to complete each sentence. Write the letters.

_c_ 1. Anna gives advice to people

____ 2. Jamie writes to Anna

____ 3. We think our friends will tell us the truth

____ 4. We may not always want to hear the truth

____ 5. Maybe Anna won't have a good answer

a. because we trust them.

b. because the question is difficult.

c. because that is her job.

d. because the truth can hurt.

e. because he has a question for her.

Reading for Details

Read the statements. Circle True or False. Circle "It doesn't say" if the reading does not give that information.

1. Jamie puts only his first name at the end of his letter.　　True　　False　　It doesn't say.

2. Jamie's friend knows that Jamie is writing to Anna for advice.　　True　　False　　It doesn't say.

3. Jamie's friend worries about hurting a friend's feelings.　　True　　False　　It doesn't say.

4. Jamie and his friend go to school together.　　True　　False　　It doesn't say.

5. The writer says that sometimes it's better to lie to your friends.　　True　　False　　It doesn't say.

6. The writer says you should never be afraid to hear the truth.　　True　　False　　It doesn't say.

7. The writer agrees with Jamie.　　True　　False　　It doesn't say.

CRITICAL THINKING

Discussion

Talk about these questions with your class.

1. In Jamie's letter, look again at the sentence that begins "This is what it means to be a friend." What does "this" mean? What does it mean to "be open with" somebody? Compare Jamie's definition of a friend with the dictionary definition on page 93. How are they different? Which definition do you think is better? Why?

2. In paragraph 2, who does the writer agree with, Jamie or Jamie's friend? Underline the part of the reading that gives you the answer. Why does the writer say we should tell our friends the truth? Do you agree? Tell why or why not.

3. Look again at the question that begins paragraph 3. Would the writer answer this question "Yes" or "No"? Underline the parts of paragraph 3 that tell you what the writer's answer would be.

4. Read paragraph 4 again. Why would the friend feel hurt? Why would the friend feel angry? In this paragraph, do you think the writer agrees with Jamie or with Jamie's friend? Why?

5. A friend of yours is doing something that seems like a bad idea. Would you tell your friend your opinion, or would you wait for your friend to ask, "What do you think?" What would Jamie do? What would Jamie's friend do?

6. How do you think Anna will answer Jamie? How would *you* answer Jamie?

A. Use the Target Vocabulary: Complete the sentences. Write your sentences on a piece of paper. Then find a partner, and read each other's sentences.

1. It's **difficult** to _________________________________.

2. You **should** never _________________________________.

3. I sometimes **worry** about _________________________________.

4. I sometimes get **angry** when _________________________________.

5. Here's my advice: It's **better** to _______________ than to _______________.

B. Writing Practice: Choose sentence 1 or 2. Copy it on a piece of paper. Add three or more sentences with your reasons to make a paragraph. Then find a partner, and read each other's paragraph.

1. I think that you should always tell your friends the truth.

2. I don't think that you can always tell your friends the truth.

> **Writing Tip:** Use *should (not)* + the base form of a verb to say you think something is (or is not) a good idea: *They should be careful. You shouldn't worry.*

CHAPTER 12

Are Online Friends *Real* Friends?

LEARNING OUTCOME

> Learn about different opinions on the topic of online friends

GETTING READY TO READ

Talk about these questions with your class.

1. What does the phrase *online friend* mean?

2. Some people make online friends by using social networking websites. Check (✓) the ones in this list that you know something about.

   ☐ Google+   ☐ Facebook   ☐ Twitter   ☐ Qzone
   ☐ Instagram   ☐ Sina Weibo   ☐ VK   ☐ LinkedIn

   Which sites do the most people in the class know something about? What other important social networking websites can you and your classmates name?

Read to Find Out: Who are Kris and Jaden, and what are their opinions?

Look at the words and definitions next to the reading. Then read. Do not stop to use a dictionary.

Are Online Friends *Real* Friends?

1   Are online friends *real* friends? A teacher asked her students to write their answers to that question. Here is what two students, Kris and Jaden, had to say.

2   Kris wrote, "For me, online friends are real friends. My online friends are really important in my life! We talk about everything. When I say "talk," I mean we chat[1] online. We don't talk on the phone, and they don't live near me, so we don't talk in person.[2] We met[3] online because we're **interested in** the same things. First we talked about music and movies. Then we started telling **each other** about our lives. I feel I can tell them anything. They tell me about their families, their problems, their hopes for the **future**. That's what makes us **close**. I know some people say online friends aren't *real* friends, but I say they're **wrong**. They say it's **too** hard to know who you can trust online. That may be true sometimes, but it can be hard in person, too."

3   Jaden wrote, "I know that online friends are important to many people. They talk to each other about what's **going on** in their lives, and that's a big part of being friends. But I think it's a **mistake** to call online friends *real* friends. You need to be careful when you **choose** your friends. Is it really **safe** to trust people online? Are they telling you the truth? Or do they say only the things you want to hear? That's not what real friends do. I also think you have to get to know[4] people in real life before you really know who they are, and you need to be careful when you plan to meet in person. I'm not as close to my online friends as my real-life friends. But a few of my real-life friends I met online first. Then we met in person. After spending some time together, we became[5] *real* friends."

[1] *chat* = write messages to each other online

[2] *in person* = doing something face-to-face with other people

[3] *met* = the simple past tense form of *meet*

[4] *get to know* = learn about (a person, place, etc.)

[5] *became* = started to be

Quick Comprehension Check

A. Read these sentences **about the reading**. Circle T (true) or F (false). On the line, write the number of the paragraph with the answer.

1. Kris and Jaden are students in the same class.   T   F   ____

2. Their teacher asked them to write about online   T   F   ____
   friends.

3. Kris has online friends, but Jaden does not.   T   F   ____

4. They agree that online friends are real friends.   T   F   ____

5. Jaden sometimes meets online friends   T   F   ____
   face-to-face.

B. Work with your class. Share your answers from part A. Go back to the reading to show why a sentence is true or false. Correct the false sentences.

EXPLORING VOCABULARY

Thinking about the Target Vocabulary

A. Find the words in **bold** in "Are Online Friends *Real* Friends?" on page 109. Write them in the list. Use alphabetical order.

1. _____*choose*_____   6. _______________

2. _______________   7. _______________

3. _______________   8. _______________

4. _______________   9. _______________

5. _______________   10. _______________

B. Circle the words in the list that are new to you. Find those words in the reading. Can you guess their meanings?

Understanding the Target Vocabulary

A. Complete the sentences with the words and phrases in the box. The sentences are **about the reading**.

choose	close	future	going on	interested in	too

1. Online friends often like and want to talk about the same kinds of

   things. They are _______________ the same things.

2. Kris's online friends talk about their hopes for the _______________ : the

   things they hope will happen next week, next month, and in the years to come.

3. When people have friends that they know very well and care a lot about,

    these are their _________________ friends.

4. Some people tell Kris that they don't know whom to trust online. It is so

    difficult for them that they cannot do it. It is _________________ hard.

5. Jaden says that talking about what is happening in your life is "a

    big part of being friends." We want our friends to know what is

    _________________ in our lives.

6. Jaden says you need to decide on the right people to trust as

    friends. You should be careful when you _________________ your

    friends.

B. Complete the sentences about the pictures. Write *each other, mistake, safe,* or *wrong.*

1. There's a _________________ on the paper.

2. His shoes are on the _________________ feet.

3. They love _________________.

4. Use your seatbelt to be _________________.

C. Complete the conversations with the words in the box.

close	safe	mistake	too	wrong

1. A: Are you and your sister _________________?

    B: Yes, she's my best friend! We talk on the phone every day.

2. **A:** Can people drink the water from the river?

   B: No, it's not _________________. It'll make you sick.

3. **A:** Hello, may I please speak to Maria?

   B: Maria? There's no Maria here. You called the _________________

   number.

4. **A:** Are you going to swim?

   B: No, the water's _________________ cold for me!

5. **A:** Please don't marry him. He's not the right man for you.

   B: You think I'm making a _________________?

D. Complete the sentences with the words and phrases in the box.

choose	each other	future	going on	interested in

1. Good friends can trust _________________.

2. I don't want to watch the game. I'm not _________________ basketball.

3. What kind of ice cream should we buy? You _________________. I like them all.

4. Harry knows he doesn't eat enough vegetables. He says he's going to eat

   more in the _________________.

5. She's very busy. There's a lot _________________ in her life.

DEVELOPING YOUR READING SKILLS

The Topic and the Main Idea

A. Go back to page 109 and read "Are Online Friends *Real* Friends?" again.

B. Answer the questions about the topic and the main idea of the reading.

1. What is "Are Online Friends *Real* Friends?" about? Check (✔) the topic.

   ☐ a. going online

   ☐ b. student's opinions

   ☐ c. friends

2. What does the reading say about the topic? Check (✔) the main idea.

    ☐ a. You should be careful about trusting people you know only online.

    ☐ b. Some people think online friends are real friends, but others don't.

    ☐ c. What makes people friends is talking about each other's lives.

Pronoun Reference

That as a Pronoun

Pronouns are words like *we, it, they,* and *them. That* can also be a pronoun. We sometimes use *that* when we don't want to repeat an idea.

> *That*
> The teacher asked, "Are online friends real friends?" ~~The question "Are online friends real friends?"~~ is an interesting question.

When you see *that* as a pronoun in a reading, it's important to know what idea the writer is talking about.

What does the pronoun *that* mean in each of these sentences? Look back at the reading on page 109. Write the answers.

1. Paragraph 2: That's what makes us close. _______________________________

2. Paragraph 2: That may be true sometimes . . . _______________________________

3. Paragraph 3: . . . and that's a big part of being friends. _______________________________

4. Paragraph 3: That's not what real friends do. _______________________________

Sentences with *Because*

Complete the sentences with *because.* Use information from the reading.

1. Kris met some people online because they are ________________ the same things.

2. Kris feels that online friends are real friends because they

    ____.

3. Some people say online friends cannot be real friends because you

    don't know ____.

4. Jaden doesn't think ____ because you have to get to know people in real life.

5. Some of Jaden's online friends are now real friends because ________________

    ____.

> **Reading Tip:** Sometimes the pronoun *you* means the person who is listening or reading, and sometimes it means "anyone, everyone."

CRITICAL THINKING

Discussion

Talk about these questions in a small group.

1. How did Kris's online friendships begin, and how did they change? Underline the parts of the reading that help you answer this question.

2. Read paragraph 2 again. How do you think Kris would answer the question "What is a friend?" Read paragraph 3 again. How do you think Jaden would answer the same question? Do Kris and Jaden agree?

3. What do Kris and Jaden disagree about? What reasons does each person give? Complete the T-chart. Then tell who you think is right and why.

> **Critical Thinking Tip:** Making a T-chart can help you understand and remember two different opinions on a topic, or a list of pros and cons.

Where Kris and Jaden Disagree	
Kris thinks:	Jaden thinks:

WRITING

A. Use the Target Vocabulary: Complete the sentences. Write your sentences on a piece of paper. Then find a partner, and read each other's sentences.

1. I'm **interested in** learning about ___________________________.

2. In the **future**, I want to ___________________________.

3. Friends should ___________________________ **each other**.

4. The people I'm **close** to are ___________________________.

5. It's not **safe** to ___________________________.

B. Writing Practice: Choose sentence 1 or sentence 2 below to use as the first sentence of a paragraph. Add three or more reasons to support the sentence. Then find a partner and read each other's paragraph.

1. I think online friends can be real friends.

2. I don't think online friends are the same as real friends.

> **Writing Tip:** The first sentence in your paragraph gives the main idea. Your other sentences should all support that sentence and show why your main idea is true.

Checkpoint

LOOK BACK

A. Think About This

Look back at how you completed the *Think About This* sentence on page 91:

A friend is someone who . . .

Would you like to change or add anything?

B. Remember the Readings

What do you want to remember from the readings in Unit 4? For each chapter, write one sentence about the reading.

Chapter 10: Good Friends and Good Health

____

Chapter 11: Being Honest with Friends

____

Chapter 12: Are Online Friends *Real* Friends?

____

REVIEWING VOCABULARY

Write the correct word to complete the sentence.

1. I think you're going to have a great _______________!
   - a. mistake
   - b. worry
   - c. future

2. I love my brother. We're very _______________ friends.
   - a. wrong
   - b. difficult
   - c. close

3. Go slowly and be _______________ when you drive in bad weather.
   - a. angry
   - b. careful
   - c. should

4. Sam and Pat are happily married. They love _______________.
   - a. tell the truth
   - b. each other
   - c. interested in

5. Call me _______________ you need help.
   - a. safe
   - b. strong
   - c. if

6. Don't tell her we're coming—we want to _______________ her.
   - a. surprise
   - b. trust
   - c. choose

7. My grandmother is 90, but she's in good _______________.
   - a. life
   - b. heart
   - c. health

8. There is too much _______________ in my life—I'm too busy!
   - a. going on
   - b. getting better
   - c. understanding

9. Be careful not to say anything to _______________ her feelings.
   - a. hurt
   - b. better
   - c. sad

10. I _______________ see your brother, but I never see you.
    - a. too
    - b. often
    - c. so

EXPANDING VOCABULARY

Verbs

There are many different kinds of words. A noun is one kind of word. You learned about nouns on page 86.

A **verb** is a kind of word, too. Every sentence needs a verb.

What Is a Verb?		Examples of Verbs
A verb is a word for	an action:	He **runs** every day. Let's **go**. They**'re working**.
	a feeling or a state:	Everyone **is** ready. I **feel** fine. **Do** you **know** John?

A verb can have many forms: *talk, talks,* and *talked,* for example.

A verb can also have more than one part: *don't talk, is talking,* and *can talk,* for example.

Each sentence has a verb. Find and circle the verb.

1. (Catch) the ball!
2. I often use the Internet.
3. He never wears a hat.
4. Children grow quickly.
5. My mother enjoys love stories.
6. I agree with you.
7. They have a small boat.
8. I don't understand the homework.
9. They can't decide on a name for the baby.
10. Fruit is a good snack.
11. Please remember the date.
12. Don't worry.

A PUZZLE

Complete these sentences with words you studied in Chapters 10–12. Look at the word lists on pages 92, 102, and 110 for help. Write the words in the puzzle.

ACROSS

1. After running, my h_______________ beats faster.

4. The kids are tired. They s_______________ go to bed.

7. Don't swim there! It's not s_______________.

10. I'll go i_______________ you'll come too.

11. I can't wear these shoes. They're t_______________ small.

13. He's a runner, so he has s_______________ legs.

14. I hope you will live a long l_______________.

DOWN

1. Eating well is good for your h_______________.

2. She's a_______________ because I didn't tell the truth.

3. Our friends are people we t_______________.

5. It's not easy. It's d_______________.

6. I'm afraid I'm making a m_______________.

7. It's late, s_______________ we should go now.

8. With 20 kinds of ice cream, I don't know which to c_______________!

9. I got on the w_______________ bus by mistake.

12. We'll be safe. You don't need to w_______________ about us.

Pets as Friends

1. A pet is an animal you care about and are responsible for.[1] Cats, dogs, and fish are the favorite pets in the United States. In Brazil, people love dogs. No country in the world has more dogs than Brazil. The most popular[2] pet in Russia is the cat, and in China, it's the cricket.

2. For many people, pets are part of the family. For some, a pet is their closest friend. But can a pet really be a friend?

A cricket

3. We know that human[3] friends are good for us. They're good for our health, they help us live longer, and they make us happier. They make us feel good by listening to what's going on in our lives. Can pets do all that? Yes, it seems that they can.

4. Researchers[4] in the United States study people who have pets they feel close to. They say there are three ways that pets are good for people.

   - People with pets don't feel as much stress.[5]

   - People who have health problems (with their heart, for example) do better if they have a pet.

   - When bad things happen, pets help their owners feel better faster than people without pets.

5. Some people may disagree that a pet can be a real friend. They might say, "Pets are important only to people with no human friends!" The researchers say no, that's not true. They say most people who love a pet also have good human friends.

---

1. *you are responsible for = you have to take care of*
2. *popular = liked by a lot of people*
3. *human = relating to people (not animals)*
4. *researchers = people whose job is to study a subject to learn new facts or test ideas*
5. *stress = feelings of worry that stop you from relaxing*

Comprehension Check

Read these sentences about the reading. Circle T (true) or F (false). On the line, write the number of the paragraph with the answer.

1. Cats and dogs are popular pets.   T   F   _____

2. Many people think of their pets like family or friends.   T   F   _____

3. Taking care of a pet makes people worry more about their lives.   T   F   _____

4. Pets make life more difficult for people with health problems.   T   F   _____

5. People who love their pets don't have many human friends.   T   F   _____

Sentences with *Because*

Complete each sentence with *because*. Use information from the reading.

1. People need to take care of their pets because ________________________________

    ____

    ____.

2. Spending time with your friends is good for you because ________________________

    ____

    ____.

3. Researchers know that a pet can be good for you because they ___________________

    ____

    ____.

4. People with pets may not worry as much because people with pets ________________

    ____

    ____.

5. Pets are like human friends because they__________________________________

    ____

    ____.

The Topic and the Main Idea

1. What is "Pets as Friends" about? Check (✔) the topic.
    - ☐ a. favorite pets in different countries
    - ☐ b. people and their pets
    - ☐ c. different opinions about pets

2. What does the reading say about the topic? Check (✔) the main idea.
    - ☐ a. For many people, their closest friend is their pet.
    - ☐ b. Pets are good for people, like human friends are.
    - ☐ c. People have different opinions about kinds of pets.

Critical Thinking

Talk about these questions with your class.

1. Does any information in paragraph 1 surprise you? Tell why or why not. How do the favorite pets in the United States, Brazil, Russia, and China compare with the favorite pets in your country? (If you can, look online to learn about the numbers of different kinds of pets in your country.)

2. Circle the words the writer used in these sentences from paragraph 2.

"For

everyone with a pet,
most people,
many people,
some people,

pets are part of the family. For

everyone with a pet,
most,
many,
some,

their pet is their closest friend."

   Do you agree with the writer, or would you choose different words? Give the reasons for your answers.

3. Go back and read "Good Friends and Good Health" on page 91. Then read paragraphs 3 and 4 of "Pets as Friends" here. What does research show is the same for human friends and pets?

4. In paragraph 2, the writer asks, "But can a pet really be a friend?" How does the writer answer that question? How well do the definitions for *friend* on pages 91 and 93 work when you think about pets as friends? How would you answer the question, "But can a pet really be a friend?"

Vocabulary Self-Test 2

Choose an answer to complete each sentence. Circle the letter of your answer.

1. You have to run to _____________ the ball.
   a. understand   b. catch   c. trust

2. I tell my friends what's _____________ in my life.
   a. getting   b. standing   c. going on

3. Call me _____________ you need anything.
   a. without   b. if   c. often

4. _____________ player wears a different number.
   a. Both   b. Together   c. Each

5. China has more people than any other country in the _____________.
   a. field   b. world   c. heart

6. Please _____________ not to laugh!
   a. try   b. beat   c. hold

7. They have flowers all _____________ their house.
   a. around   b. each other   c. too

8. No, this isn't 555-2000; you have the _____________ number.
   a. wrong   b. safe   c. only

9. Ask a doctor when you have questions about your _____________.
   a. team   b. health   c. choose

10. That _____________ expensive to me. What do you think?
    a. cares   b. laughs   c. seems

11. We need to _____________ what to do about this problem.
    a. decide   b. enjoy   c. pick up

12. He thinks it's too difficult, and I _____________ with him.
    a. surprise   b. continue   c. agree

13. I do crossword puzzles in pencil, not pen, because I make many
______________.

   a. futures   b. rules   c. mistakes

14. I'm sorry, but I don't ______________ your name.

   a. hurt   b. collect   c. remember

15. Mothers and fathers often ______________ about their children.

   a. should   b. strong   c. worry

16. That store is closed, ______________ we can't shop there.

   a. somewhere   b. so   c. close

17. Please be ______________ when you pick up the baby.

   a. careful   b. angry   c. sad

18. We need two people to ______________ the TV.

   a. carry   b. hope   c. happen

See the Answer Key on page 159.

ON THE JOB

THINK ABOUT THIS

Think about a job you would like. What is most important to you?

Number your answers from 1 (most important) to 4 (not so important). Add your own ideas.

- What you do at work
- Where you work
- When you work
- Who you work with
- Your idea:

CHAPTER 13

Working Teens

A teen[1] at work

LEARNING OUTCOME

❯ Learn about high school students with jobs

GETTING READY TO READ

Talk about these questions with your class.

1. Look at the photo. What do you see?

2. What kinds of jobs do teenagers do? List some jobs or some places where they might work.

3. In your opinion, what is a good age to start working?

[1] *a teen* = a teenager, a person who is 13–19 years old

READING

Read to Find Out: When do U.S. teenagers usually start working?

Look at the words next to the reading. Then read. Do not stop to use a dictionary.

Working Teens

1 Is it a good idea for teenagers to work before they finish high school?[1] Some people say yes, teenagers should work, but others say no, they should not. **Let's** read four opinions.

Jeff Baker, father: Teenagers are **expensive**! I want my kid[2] to get a job.

Wendy Tajima, mother: I think kids today work too much.

Don Robbins, teacher: High school students should be studying, not working.

April Baker, teenager: It's my life! I'll work if I want to!

2 Let's look at some **facts** about working teens in the United States. Many U.S. high school students have jobs. More than **half** of all U.S. teenagers start working before they are 15 years old. Some work only in the summer, but most work **during** the school year, too. Some high school students work full-time.[3]

3 There are good reasons for teenagers to work. They can learn things on the job that they cannot learn in school. **Making money** feels good, too. Some teenagers use the money to help their **parents**, and some **save** it for college.

4 There are also good reasons for teenagers *not* to work. Working takes time, and they may need that time to do schoolwork and to get enough sleep. They also need time to build **relationships**. The fact is, studies[4] show that working more than 20 hours a week is bad for high school students. It's bad for their schoolwork and also for relationships **between** teenagers and their families and friends.

5 Maybe you can think of more reasons why high school students should or should not work. What's your opinion on the question?

[1] *high school =* (in the U.S.) grades 9–12, for students usually aged 13–18

[2] *my kid =* my son or daughter

[3] *full-time =* 35 or more hours a week

[4] *studies =* research work done to learn something and write reports about it

[5] *the fact is =* the real truth is

Quick Comprehension Check

A. Read these sentences **about the reading**. Circle T (true) or F (false). On the line, write the number of the paragraph with the answer.

1. A lot of high school students in the United States have jobs.   T   F   _____

2. Everyone in the United States thinks work is good for teenagers.   T   F   _____

3. U.S. teenagers usually start work when they are 16 or older.   T   F   _____

4. Some teenagers help their families by working.   T   F   _____

5. Working can be a bad idea for teenagers.   T   F   _____

B. Work with your class. Share your answers from part A. Go back to the reading to show why a sentence is true or false. Correct the false sentences.

EXPLORING VOCABULARY

Thinking about the Target Vocabulary

A. Find the words in **bold** in "Working Teens" on page 127. Write them in the list. Use alphabetical order.

1. _____between_____
2. _______________
3. _______________
4. _______________
5. _______________
6. _______________
7. _______________
8. _______________
9. _______________
10. _______________

B. Circle the words in the list that are new to you. Find those words in the reading. Can you guess their meanings?

Understanding The Target Vocabulary

A. Complete the sentences with the words in the box. The sentences are **about the reading**.

during	expensive	fact	let's	make money	relationships	save

1. The writer says "_________________ read four opinions," the opinions of

   a father, a mother, a teacher, and a teenager. The writer means "I want us

   to read together."

2. The father says, "Teenagers are ________________!" He means that he

    spends a lot of money on his teenaged son or daughter.

3. Many U.S. high school students work. That is a ________________. That

    is a piece of information that is true.

4. Most U.S. teenagers with jobs work in the summer and also

    ________________ the school year—from September to June.

5. When teenagers have jobs, someone pays them to work. They

    ________________ when they work.

6. Some teenagers put the money they make in the bank. They don't spend

    it; they ________________ it.

7. We are connected to family and friends. We have ________________ with

    them.

B. Complete the sentences about the pictures. Write *between, half,* or *parents.*

1. Would you like ________________ of my apple?

2. That's me, and those are my ________________.

3. The post office is ________________ the bank and
    the police station.

C. Complete the sentences with the words in the box.

during	facts	half	make . . . money	parents	saving

1. Please do not use your cell phone ________________ class.

2. Do you look like your ________________?

3. The children seem to be learning a lot of ________________ about the sun.

4. ________________ of the students work: 11 out of 22 students have jobs.

5. I want to get a better job, a job where I can ________________ more

   ________________.

6. I'm ________________ my money. In the future, I want to buy a car.

D. Complete the conversations with the words in the box.

between	expensive	let's	relationship

1. A: Are you going to buy those shoes?

   B: No, they're too ________________.

2. A: I need to learn to use all these new words.

   B: So do I. ________________ practice them together.

3. A: Do you think Luis is a good father?

   B: Yes, he has a great ________________ with his son.

4. A: Do you want to get something to eat ________________ classes?

   B: Yes, let's do that. I'm free from 11:00 to 12:00. How about you?

DEVELOPING YOUR READING SKILLS

The Topic and the Main Idea

A. Go back to page 127 and read "Working Teens" again.

B. Answer the questions about the topic and the main idea of the reading.
1. What is "Working Teens" about? Check (✔) the topic.
   - ☐ a. High school students and work
   - ☐ b. Teenagers and money
   - ☐ c. Good jobs for teens

2. What is another good title for the reading? Check (✔) the title that gives
the main idea.

    ☐ a. Should High School Students Have Jobs?

    ☐ b. How Much Do Teenagers Work?

    ☐ c. Who Wants Teens to Work?

Reading for Details

Complete the sentences with information from the reading.

1. People have different _________________ about teens and work.

2. Many _________________ students in the United States have jobs.

3. More than 50 percent of all U.S. teenagers start working before they are

   _________________ years old.

4. Most teens with jobs work in the summer and during _________________, too.

5. There are good _________________ for teenagers to work—and for them not

   to work, too.

6. Studies show that teens should not work more than _________________ hours

   a week during the school year.

Fact vs. Opinion

How Facts and Opinions Are Different

A fact is information you can show is true. For example, it's a fact that "basketball is a sport." It's easy for everyone to agree that this is true. But "basketball is more fun to watch than soccer" is an opinion. Some people think this is true, but it's not true for everyone.

Does each sentence state a fact or give an opinion? Write *fact* or *opinion* on the line.

1. Teenagers are expensive.   *opinion*

2. Many U.S. high school students have jobs.   *fact*

3. High school students should not work.   _______________

4. Some teens work only in the summer.   _______________

5. Some teens make money to help their families.   _______________

6. High school students do not study enough.   _______________

7. Teens cannot get enough sleep if they work.   _______________

8. Studies show that working can be bad for teens.   _______________

CRITICAL THINKING

Discussion

Talk about these questions in a small group.

1. In paragraph 1, four people give opinions. Who agrees with whom? What do you think April means: Is she saying that she wants to work or that she doesn't want to? Why do you think so?

2. What reasons should go in each part of the T-chart below? Use information from the reading.

The Pros and Cons of Jobs for High School Students	
Reasons for High School Students to Work	Reasons for High School Students *Not* to Work
1.	1.
2.	2.
3.	3.

3. The main question in this reading is, "Is it a good idea for teenagers to work before they finish high school?" What do you think the writer's answer is? Why?

4. Read these opinions. Do you agree? Check (✔) your answers and talk about your reasons for agreeing or disagreeing.

Opinions	I agree.	I disagree.
1. Teenagers are expensive for their parents.	☐	☐
2. It's good for high school students to work.	☐	☐
3. Some things are more important than work for teenagers.	☐	☐
4. Teenagers should decide when and if they will work.	☐	☐

WRITING

A. Use the Target Vocabulary: Complete the sentences. Write your sentences on a piece of paper. Then find a partner, and read each other's sentences.

1. I would like to ________________________ every day **during** the summer.

2. I want to **make** enough **money** to ________________________.

3. A good **parent** always ________________________.

4. ________________________ is **between** ________________________ and ________________________.

5. **Let's** ________________________

B. Writing Practice: On a piece of paper, write a paragraph about high school students and work. Give your opinion and your reasons for it. You can begin:

In my opinion, it (is / is not) a good idea for high school students to work.

After you finish your paragraph, give it a title.

Example:

In my opinion, it is a good idea for teenagers to work a little during high school. It is good because they can get experience. They can learn …

> **Writing Tip:** When you write your opinion, give reasons to support it (to show why it's a good opinion).

CHAPTER 14

Night Work

Construction workers on the night shift

LEARNING OUTCOME

❯ Learn about people who work at night

GETTING READY TO READ

Talk about these questions with your class.

1. Look at the photo. What do you see?
2. What hours do most people work?
3. What time of day or night do you like to go to sleep?
4. An owl is a kind of bird. Some people are called "night owls." What do you think that means?

Read to Find Out: What are the pros and cons of working at night?

Look at the words and pictures next to the reading. Then read. Do not stop to use a dictionary.

Night Work

1. Most workers work during the day and sleep at night, but not everyone does that: some people work at night. In the United States, for example, there are more than 15 million[1] night workers.

2. We need night workers in our 24/7 world, but working at night may be bad for the people who do it. Here are three reasons to worry about working at night.

3. • Many night workers don't sleep well during the day. Because they don't, they feel tired at night, and then they make mistakes, or they **forget** things. Night workers have more **accidents**, too, and if they work with **machines**, they can get hurt.

4. • Night workers have to eat, but our **bodies** are made for eating during the day, not at night. People are not like bats![2] So eating at night can give a person problems with his or her digestive system.[3]

5. • Night workers often do not see much of their friends and families. Working the night **shift** sometimes **means** that husbands and wives don't have enough time together. It can hurt their relationship and make their home life difficult. In the United States, many night workers get divorced.[4]

6. With all these problems, why do people work at night? Some people do it because they have to. Others choose to do it because they can make more money at night or because they want to be home with their children during the day. Some people do it because they are happier doing things at night. These are the people we call "night owls."

7. Donna Smith is a night owl, and she loves working the night shift at her **company**. She starts work at 9:00 p.m. and **leaves** to go home at 6:00 a.m. Donna says, "Working the night shift is great. All the bosses[5] are home in bed. We work **hard** but without the **stress**."

[1] *15 million =* 15,000,000

[2] *a bat*

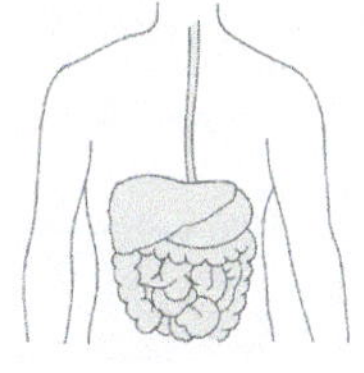

[3] *the digestive system*

[4] *get divorced =* stop being married

[5] *the boss =* the person who tells workers what to do

Quick Comprehension Check

A. Read these sentences **about the reading**. Circle T (true) or F (false). On the line, write the number of the paragraph with the answer.

1. Many U.S. workers work at night and sleep during the day. T F _____

2. The reading says that working at night is good for you. T F _____

3. Night workers sometimes make mistakes because they are tired. T F _____

4. Night work can make life hard for married people. T F _____

5. Night owls are people who sleep well at night. T F _____

B. Work with your class. Share your answers from part A. Go back to the reading to show why a sentence is true or false. Correct the false sentences.

EXPLORING VOCABULARY

Thinking about the Target Vocabulary

A. Find the words in **bold** in "Night Work" on page 135. Write them in the list. Use alphabetical order.

1. _accidents_
2. _______________
3. _______________
4. _______________
5. _______________
6. _______________
7. _______________
8. _______________
9. _______________
10. _______________

B. Circle the words in the list that are new to you. Find those words in the reading. Can you guess their meanings?

Understanding the Target Vocabulary

A. Complete the sentences with the words in the box. The sentences are **about the reading**.

company	forget	hard	leaves	means	shift	stress

1. It's hard to remember things if you don't get enough sleep. When night

   workers are tired, they _________________ things.

2. A _________________ is the period of time—usually 8–12 hours— that a group of workers are on the job.

3. The writer says, "Working the night shift sometimes _________________ that husbands and wives don't have enough time together." Working the night shift sometimes has that result.

4. Donna Smith works for a business. It's a _________________ that makes computers.

5. Donna arrives at work before 9:00 p.m. She finishes work at 6:00 a.m., so she _________________ at 6:00 and goes home.

6. Donna tries to do her job well. She works _________________.

7. Many people don't like to work with the boss watching them. It makes them worry. It causes _________________.

B. Complete the sentences about the pictures. Write *accident*, *body*, or *machine*.

1. This is a sewing _________________.

2. George had a car _________________.

3. How many parts of the _________________ can you name?

C. Complete the sentences with the words in the box.

body	leave	machines	shift	stress

1. Cars, computers, and airplanes are all _________________.

2. Your head, hands, legs, and feet are all parts of your _________________.

3. When the class ends, the students _________________.

4. Yuri works the night _________________ at the hospital. He

   starts work at 11:00 p.m.

> **Vocabulary Tip:** You can use *leave* alone or use *leave* + a place: *When the class ends, the students leave the classroom.*

5. When I think about everything I have to do, I feel a lot of

   _________________.

D. Complete the conversations with the words in the box.

accident	company	forget	hard	mean

1. A: Don't _________________: There's no class on Friday.

   B: Don't worry, I'll remember!

2. A: What _________________ does she work for?

   B: I forget the name, but they make computers.

3. A: The tickets for the game are really expensive.

   B: Does this _________________ you don't want to go?

4. A: She says she isn't doing well in school.

   B: I think she's just not trying _________________ enough.

5. A: What happened?

   B: It was an _________________.

DEVELOPING YOUR READING SKILLS

The Topic and the Main Idea

A. Go back to page 135 and read "Night Work" again.

B. Answer the questions about the topic and the main idea of the reading.

1. What is "Night Work" about? Check (✔) the topic.
   - ☐ a. Reasons we need night workers
   - ☐ b. Different kinds of night work
   - ☐ c. People who work at night

2. What is another good title for the reading? Check (✔) the title that gives the main idea.
   - ☐ a. How to Find a Good Night Job
   - ☐ b. Five Good Reasons to Work at Night
   - ☐ c. A Few Facts about Working at Night

Reading for Details

A. Complete the answers to the questions.

1. How many night workers are there in the United States? There are

   _______________.

2. Who is Donna Smith? She is _______________.

3. What hours does Donna Smith work? She works from _______________.

4. Why does she work at night? She is _______________.

5. Who is "home in bed" at night? _______________ are.

B. Complete the T-chart. Use information from the reading.

Pros and Cons of Night Work	
Reasons Some People Work at Night	Reasons Not to Work at Night
1.	1.
2.	2.
3.	3.

Fact vs. Opinion

Does each sentence state a fact or give an opinion? Write *fact* or *opinion* on the line.

1. Working at night is fun. _______________

2. Millions of people in the United States work at night. _______________

3. Most people work during the day. _______________

4. Some people work at night to make more money. _______________

5. Night owls are often happier doing things at night. _______________

6. Working the night shift is easy. _______________

7. Night workers feel more stress than other people. _______________

8. Working at night might be a bad idea. _______________

CRITICAL THINKING

Discussion

Talk about these questions with your class.

1. The reading says, "We need night workers in our 24/7 world." What do 24, 7, and "our 24/7 world" mean? List some examples of the kinds of night workers we need.

2. The reading lists "reasons to worry about working at night." Which reason do you think is most important? Why? The reading also lists reasons why people agree to work at night, even knowing about the problems that may come with the job. Which reason is most important?

3. Donna Smith speaks about stress at work. What is stress? In Donna's opinion, where does stress at work come from? Do you agree that this is the number one cause of stress at work?

4. What definition of a night owl do you find in the reading? Are you a night owl? Tell why or why not.

5. Was any of the information in the reading new to you? Did this reading change your thinking in any way about working at night or the people who work at night? What do you think about working at night yourself?

> **Reading Tip:** The writer **quotes** Donna. This means the writer uses Donna's words, with quotation marks (" ") before and after them. A writer usually quotes someone because the person knows a lot about a topic.

WRITING

A. Use the Target Vocabulary: Complete the sentences. Write your sentences on a piece of paper. Then find a partner, and read each other's sentences.

1. I usually **leave** for _________________ at _________________.

2. People have **accidents** when they _________________________.

3. I sometimes **forget** _________________________________.

4. I work **hard** to _______________________________________.

5. I feel **stress** when __________________________________.

> **Writing Tip:** Use *leave for* + the place you are going to: *The children leave for school at 8:00 a.m.*

B. Writing Practice: Think about your answers to the questions. Then write a short paragraph with your answers on a piece of paper. After you finish your paragraph, give it a title.

1. Are you a morning person or a night owl?
2. Do you like to go to bed early or stay up late?
3. Do you like to get up early or sleep late?
4. What is your favorite time of day or night to do homework?

Example:

I am a morning person. I like to go to bed early. I usually go to bed at 9:30 p.m. I like to get up early, too. My favorite time to do homework is . . .

CHAPTER 15

Working for Tips

Picking up a tip

GETTING READY TO READ

Talk about these questions with your class.

1. Look at the photo. What is happening?
2. Read the definition of *tip*. Then check (✔) all the people who get tips.

> **tip** /tɪp/ *noun* an amount of money that you give to someone who does a service for you

Who gets tips?

- ☐ waiters
- ☐ teachers
- ☐ taxi drivers
- ☐ bus drivers
- ☐ pizza delivery people
- ☐ salespeople

Read to Find Out: Do people in the United States agree on rules for tipping?

Look at the words next to the reading. Then read. Do not stop to use a dictionary.

Working for Tips

1   David Vargas is a waiter who works at a nice restaurant in a **large** U.S. city. The minimum wage there is **over** $10.00 an hour. That means all workers in the state[1] should get more than $10.00 an hour. David does not. He gets only $4.23 an hour from his employer.[2] That is because waiters get tips, and the minimum wage for them is different.

2   In many countries, people do not give tips, and workers there do not **expect** them. In the United States, people often give tips. They expect to tip waiters and taxi drivers, for example, and waiters and taxi drivers expect to get tips. Most of their pay comes from the tips they get, not from their employers.

3   David says, "A **fair** tip for a server[3] is 15 percent[4] of your **bill**. If a server does a really good job for you, give 20 percent. But if you are with a group of people, look at your bill. Maybe the tip is on it. Some restaurants put the tip for a large group on the bill."

4   People sometimes aren't **sure** about tipping. They ask, "Who should I tip, and how much should I tip?" You can find guidelines (or rules) for tipping on the Internet, but not everyone agrees on them. Some people **believe** tipping is wrong. Here are a few **interesting** comments[5] from an online discussion of the topic:

From Gary in Ohio:	Why should I give a bigger tip on a $30 meal than on a $20 meal? The waiter doesn't work more!
From Rudy in California:	I tip the pizza delivery kid[6] 50¢. He's just a kid.
From Fran in Georgia:	I don't believe I should have to tip people. It makes me angry. People should just do their jobs and not expect extra money from me.

5   What does David think about these comments? He says, "These people don't work for tips. They don't understand. Maybe things will **change** in the future, but that's not going to happen **soon**, and for now, people like me really need our tips."

[1] *a state* = one of the 50 parts of the United States, such as Texas or Florida

[2] *his employer* = the person or company that pays him to work

[3] *server* = another word for *waiter* or *waitress*

[4] *percent* = %

[5] *a comment* = an opinion someone says or writes

[6] *a kid* = a young person

Quick Comprehension Check

A. Read these sentences **about the reading**. Circle T (true) or F (false). On the line, write the number of the paragraph with the answer.

1. David Vargas owns a restaurant. T F _____
2. Waiters in U.S. restaurants usually get tips. T F _____
3. David thinks tipping is a bad idea. T F _____
4. David thinks tips are not really important. T F _____
5. You can read about tipping on the Internet. T F _____

B. Work with your class. Share your answers from part A. Go back to the reading to show why a sentence is true or false. Correct the false sentences.

EXPLORING VOCABULARY

Thinking about the Target Vocabulary

A. Find the words in **bold** in "Working for Tips" on page 143. Write them in the list. Use alphabetical order.

1. _____believe_____
2. _____________
3. _____________
4. _____________
5. _____________

6. _____________
7. _____________
8. _____________
9. _____________
10. _____________

B. Circle the words in the list that are new to you. Find those words in the reading. Can you guess their meanings?

Understanding the Target Vocabulary

A. Complete the sentences with the words in the box. The sentences are **about the reading**.

bill	change	expect	interesting	soon	sure

1. Waiters and taxi drivers in the United States ________________ tips.

   They think they will get tips.

2. At the end of a meal in a restaurant, the waiter brings the ________________

   (or the check). This paper tells how much you have to pay.

3. People sometimes don't know what to do about tipping. They aren't _________________ who or how much to tip.

4. When people talk about a topic online, their comments are sometimes _________________ to readers. That means the readers want to read more or enjoy thinking about the comments.

5. David thinks that in the future, the rules for tipping may be different. They may _________________.

6. David says that if tipping rules change, the changes will happen far in the future. They will not happen _________________.

B. Match the **boldfaced** words and their definitions. Write the letters.

____ 1. David works in a **large** city.
____ 2. He is paid **over** $4.00 an hour.
____ 3. How much is a **fair** tip?
____ 4. Some people **believe** tipping is a bad idea.

a. right, following the rules
b. more than
c. think
d. big

C. Complete the sentences with the words in the box.

believe	change	large	over	soon

1. There are _________________ 500 people working for the company.

2. I'd like a _________________ glass of water, please.

3. How will your relationship _________________ when you get married?

4. I _________________ that he works the night shift at the hospital, but I'm not sure.

5. Let's get together again _________________.

D. Complete the conversations with the words in the box.

bill	expect	fair	interesting	sure

1. A: How much is the phone _________________ this month?

   B: Over $200.

2. A: Did you like the movie?

   B: Yes, it was a very _________________ story.

3. A: What time do we need to leave for the airport?

   B: I don't know—maybe 8:00? Or 7:00? I'm not _________________.

4. A: I cooked dinner, so you wash the dishes, OK?

   B: OK, that's _________________.

5. A: Was the party a surprise?

   B: Yes! I didn't _________________ it.

DEVELOPING YOUR READING SKILLS

The Topic and the Main Idea

A. Go back to page 143 and read "Working for Tips" again.

B. Answer the questions about the topic and the main idea of the reading.
1. What is "Working for Tips" about? Check (✔) the topic.
   - ☐ a. The job of a waiter
   - ☐ b. New rules for tipping
   - ☐ c. Giving and getting tips
2. What is another good title for the reading? Check (✔) the title that gives the main idea.
   - ☐ a. A Day in the Life of a Waiter
   - ☐ b. Changing the Rules for Tipping
   - ☐ c. Facts and Opinions About Tipping

Reading for Details

A. Complete the answers to the questions.

1. What is David Vargas's job? He is a _________________.

2. How much does David get paid? He gets _________________ an hour plus tips.

3. Who expects tips in the United States? Waiters and _________________ are two examples.

4. When do some restaurants put the tip on the bill? They do it when there

   is a large ________________________.

5. Where can you read opinions about tipping? You can find comments

   ________________________.

6. Who thinks tipping is not going to change any time soon?

   ________________________ does.

B. Whose opinion is it? Write *David*, *Gary*, *Rudy*, or *Fran*.

Opinion	Speaker
1. A fair tip for a server is 15–20% of the bill.	David
2. A waiter doesn't work more to bring me a $30 meal, so why should I tip more than for a $20 meal?	
3. People shouldn't expect tips just for doing their jobs.	
4. People who work for tips need the money.	
5. Young people don't need big tips.	

Summarizing the Reading

Complete the summary of the reading. Use *agrees, believe, bill, example, expect,* or *fair.*

Some workers in the United States ________________________ tips: waiters and taxi

(1)

drivers, for ________________________. David Vargas is a waiter who says 15 to 20

(2)

percent of the ________________________ is a ________________________ tip. Not everyone

(3) (4)

________________________ about giving tips. Some people ________________________ they

(5) (6)

should not have to give tips.

CRITICAL THINKING

Discussion

Talk about these questions with your class.

1. What does *the minimum wage* mean? Underline the sentence that tells what it means where David Vargas lives. Who do you think decides what the minimum wage is? Why doesn't David's employer pay him the minimum wage? Is there a minimum wage where you live? Do people give tips to some kinds of workers where you live?

2. In paragraph 3, David says, "A fair tip for a server is 15 percent of your bill." Is this a fact or an opinion? Why? David also gives some advice. What does he say? Why do you think he says it?

3. Do Gary, Rudy, and Fran agree with David's ideas about tipping? What do they believe and why? What would David say to Gary? To Rudy? To Fran? What would you say?

> **Reading Tip:** Look for definitions of new words when you read. Sometimes the writer will give a definition inside parentheses, as in "guidelines (or rules) for tipping" in paragraph 4.

WRITING

A. Use the Target Vocabulary: Complete the sentences. Write your sentences on a piece of paper. Then find a partner, and read each other's sentences.

1. I have to pay my _______________________________ **bill**.

2. I have to pay **over** _________________ for _________________.

3. I'm going to _______________________________ sometime **soon**.

4. I'm **sure** that _______________________________.

5. It's not **fair** when _______________________________.

B. Writing Practice: On a piece of paper, write a paragraph about giving or working for tips. Give your opinion and your reasons for it. After you finish your paragraph, give it a title.

You can begin:

In my opinion, it (is / is not) a good idea to (give / work for) tips.

Example:

> In my opinion, it is a good idea to give tips. If somebody does a good job, you give a good tip. If somebody doesn't do a good job, you don't. I think people try hard to do a good job and get a good tip.

Checkpoint

LOOK BACK

A. Think About This

Look back at your answers to the *Think About This* question on page 125:

Think about a job you would like. What is most important to you?

Would you like to change or add anything?

B. Remember the Readings

What do you want to remember from the readings in Unit 5? For each chapter, write one sentence about the reading.

Chapter 13: Working Teens

____

Chapter 14: Night Work

____

Chapter 15: Working for Tips

____

REVIEWING VOCABULARY

Write the correct word to complete the sentence.

1. It takes ________________ five hours to get there by car.
   - a. soon
   - b. over
   - c. between

2. Let's not talk ________________ the movie.
   - a. large
   - b. hard
   - c. during

3. Yes, I remember him but I ________________ his name.
   - a. mean
   - b. forget
   - c. expect

4. I can't buy it. It's too ________________.
   - a. bill
   - b. expensive
   - c. make money

5. Your arms and legs are parts of your ________________.
   - a. fact
   - b. body
   - c. parent

6. If you wash ________________ the dishes, I'll finish them.
   - a. half
   - b. fair
   - c. machine

7. I'm feeling a lot of ________________ because I have a lot of schoolwork.
   - a. shift
   - b. company
   - c. stress

8. I hope this cold, rainy weather will ________________ soon.
   - a. change
   - b. believe
   - c. save

9. What time do you ________________ for work in the morning?
   - a. leave
   - b. mean
   - c. expect

10. I think her name is Maria, but I'm not ________________.
    - a. relationship
    - b. interesting
    - c. sure

EXPANDING VOCABULARY

Adjectives

There are many different kinds of words. You know about nouns and verbs. An **adjective** is a kind of word, too. Adjectives describe people, places, things, and ideas.

Rules for Adjectives in Sentences		Examples	
		Adjective	**Noun**
1. Use adjective + noun.	They have a	**big**	house.
		beautiful	daughter.
		new	plan.
		Be/Get/Seem	**Adjective**
2. Use the verb *be, get, or seem* + adjective.	That answer	is	**wrong.**
	I'm	getting	**ready.**
	He	seems	**angry.**

Each sentence has one adjective. Find and circle the adjective.

1. I need some (extra) practice.
2. You seem tired.
3. That isn't fair!
4. Who is your favorite actor?
5. It's a difficult job.
6. Keep it in a safe place.
7. I hope you'll get rich.
8. We're studying different kinds of words.
9. That large box is for you.
10. Will the test be hard?

A PUZZLE

Complete these sentences with words you studied in Chapters 13–15. Look at the word lists on pages 128, 136, and 144 for help. Write the words in the puzzle.

ACROSS

2. Mike works with a m______________ that makes boxes.

3. Anna works the night s______________ at the hospital.

6. Dr. Lee b______________ a good breakfast is very important.

8. On my new job I will m______________ more money but have more stress, too.

9. What time do you e______________ them to get here?

10. A snack is something you eat b______________ meals.

13. We can't stay long. We have to leave s______________.

15. The police are asking for information about the a______________.

16. Where are the child's p______________?

DOWN

1. Russia is a very l______________ country.

4. What an i______________ story!

5. A friendship is the r______________ between two friends.

7. I need to s______________ money so I can buy a house.

11. *Toyota* is the name of a Japanese c______________.

12. I know I can catch the ball if I try h______________ enough.

14. Is that a f______________ or just your opinion?

EXTRA READING

Help for Working Parents

1   Olivia and Michael live and work in San Diego, California, and they are under a lot of stress. Olivia works over 40 hours a week, and Michael does, too. They believe that they don't have enough time with their children or with each other.

2   Many working men and women in the United States have the same problem. They spend too much time at work, and they worry that they cannot be good parents. "What kind of life is this?" they ask. Many say, "Something has to change!"

3   Things *are* changing, slowly. Many U.S. companies are trying to be more family-friendly[1] by making changes in the workplace. Here are three examples of the kinds of changes that are happening.

[1] *family-friendly* = helping people both work and have a family life

(continued)

4 • Some companies have flextime. This means that workers can change the times they start and end work. Some workers come in early and leave early. Others work two long days and three short days.

5 • Some companies say people can work at home part of the time. More than half of all U.S. companies with over 100 workers do this. The workers use computers and phones to do their jobs from home.

6 • Some companies say workers can job-share. Job-sharing means two workers do one job. Each worker does half the work and gets half the pay.

7 Employers[2] know that tired and unhappy workers cannot do a great job. Many employers are ready to change. It's not just good for their workers. It's good for the company, too.

[2] an *employer* = a person or company that pays a worker

Comprehension Check

Read these sentences about the reading. Circle T (true) or F (false). On the line, write the number of the paragraph with the answer.

1. Olivia and Michael are working parents.   T   F   ____
2. They have the same problem as many other parents in the U.S.   T   F   ____
3. Companies cannot change their rules to help workers.   T   F   ____
4. Some U.S. companies say their workers can work at home.   T   F   ____
5. Some U.S. workers are changing to be more family-friendly.   T   F   ____

Reading for Details

Complete these statements about the reading.

1. Olivia works ________________ hours a week.

2. Olivia and Michael want more time with ________________.

3. A lot of companies want to be more ________________.

4. "________________" means workers can change the hours they work.

5. Some companies let workers work ________________ part of the time.

6. "________________" means two workers do one job.

Fact vs. Opinion

Does each sentence state a fact or give an opinion? Write *fact* or *opinion* on the line.

1. Michael works more than 40 hours a week. _______________

2. Men who work a lot are not good fathers. _______________

3. The reading gives three examples of
    changes in the workplace. _______________

4. More companies should have flextime. _______________

5. Some U.S. companies say workers can
    work at home. _______________

6. Job-sharing is a great idea for working parents. _______________

The Main Idea

Choose another title for the reading. Check (✔) the title that gives the main idea.

- ☐ a. One Family's Problem
- ☐ b. Family-Friendly Changes in the Workplace
- ☐ c. The Future of Workers in the United States

Critical Thinking

Talk about these questions with your class.

1. What problem are Olivia and Michael having? Does the writer believe that Olivia and Michael are unusual, or does the writer believe they're like other working parents in the United States? How do you know?

2. Look at the question "What kind of life is this?" in paragraph 2. Who is asking the question? What do they mean? When they say, "Something has to change!" what kind of change do they want?

3. Read paragraphs 4, 5, and 6 again. Make notes in the chart about what each change means. Then think about what Olivia and Michael might say about each one: Is it the answer to their problem, a little helpful, or no help at all?

Flextime	
Working from home part-time	
Job-sharing	

Vocabulary Self-Test 3

Choose an answer to complete each sentence. Circle the letter of your answer.

1. We expect newspapers to give us ____________.
   a. parents   b. facts   c. meals   d. snacks

2. ____________ play Rock, Paper, Scissors!
   a. Maybe   b. Only   c. Let's   d. Would like

3. Don't worry. They'll be home ____________.
   a. sure   b. soon   c. hurt   d. difficult

4. Our class is finished, ____________ it's time to go.
   a. if   b. so   c. just   d. other

5. I can't ____________ the word.
   a. carry   b. remember   c. agree   d. hope

6. If you cut something in ____________, you have two pieces.
   a. half   b. kind   c. size   d. company

7. Everyone ____________ wash their hands before eating.
   a. get   b. should   c. too   d. use

8. I'm afraid of ____________ drivers!
   a. fair   b. favorite   c. safe   d. angry

9. I enjoy going to the movies with ____________ friends.
   a. the wrong   b. each   c. a few   d. also

10. Help! Our group is having ____________, and we don't know what to do.
    a. problems   b. details   c. examples   d. bodies

11. I hope they will have a happy ____________ together.
    a. bill   b. field   c. bowl   d. life

12. People's opinions can ____________.
    a. change   b. save   c. spend   d. forget

13. He works ______________ the day and goes to classes in the evening.
    a. because   b. over   c. between   d. during

14. They're a good team. They play ______________ together.
    a. every   b. ready   c. well   d. tired

15. Cars and computers are both ______________.
    a. chooses   b. relationships c. machines   d. laughs

16. I ______________ that is true, but I don't really know for sure.
    a. happen   b. may   c. believe   d. stand

17. We can't get the box into the car. It won't fit. It's ______________ large.
    a. enough   b. more   c. around   d. too

18. I can't swim. That ______________ I can't be on the swim team.
    a. means   b. grows   c. understands   d. trusts

19. Don't say anything to hurt his ______________.
    a. feelings   b. boxes   c. mistakes   d. shifts

20. Most teachers ______________ students to do homework.
    a. smell   b. beat   c. expect   d. collect

21. The players work ______________ at practice.
    a. without   b. expensive   c. busy   d. hard

22. Please ______________ the door open.
    a. care   b. hold   c. seem   d. continue

23. He ______________ spending time online.
    a. enjoys   b. catches   c. picks up   d. leaves

24. The parents of a new baby may be under a lot of ______________.
    a. rules   b. expensive   c. stress   d. lunch

25. We hope we will see you more often in the ______________.
    a. heart   b. accident   c. somewhere   d. future

See the Answer Key on page 159.

Vocabulary Self-Test Answer Key

Here are the answers to the Vocabulary Self-Tests. Check your answers. Then study any words you did not remember. Look for the words in the Index to Target Vocabulary on page 160. Go back to the readings and exercises with the words. Use your dictionary as needed.

Vocabulary Self-Test 1, Units 1–2 (pages 58–59)

1. c. practice	6. b. would like	11. b. busy
2. b. size	7. a. other	12. c. just
3. c. extra	8. b. too	13. a. may
4. a. most	9. b. show	14. b. a few
5. b. snack	10. c. well	15. b. details

Vocabulary Self-Test 2, Units 3–4 (pages 122–123)

1. b. catch	7. a. around	13. c. mistakes
2. c. going on	8. a. wrong	14. c. remember
3. b. if	9. b. health	15. c. worry
4. c. Each	10. c. seems	16. b. so
5. b. world	11. a. decide	17. a. careful
6. a. try	12. c. agree	18. a. carry

Vocabulary Self-Test 3, Units 1–5 (pages 156–157)

1. b. facts	10. a. problems	19. a. feelings
2. c. Let's	11. d. life	20. c. expect
3. b. soon	12. a. change	21. d. hard
4. b. so	13. d. during	22. b. hold
5. b. remember	14. c. well	23. a. enjoys
6. a. half	15. c. machines	24. c. stress
7. b. should	16. c. believe	25. d. future
8. d. angry	17. d. too	
9. c. a few	18. a. means	

Index to Target Vocabulary